Stuck in Reverse

Stuck in Reverse

How to Let God Change Your Direction

CHARLES STANLEY

THOMAS NELSON
Since 1798

NASHVILLE DALLAS MEXICO CITY RIO DE JANEIRO BEIJING

Published in Nashville, Tennessee, by Thomas Nelson. Thomas Nelson is a registered trademark of Thomas Nelson, Inc.

Thomas Nelson, Inc., titles may be purchased in bulk for educational, business, fund-raising, or sales promotional use. For information, please e-mail SpecialMarkets@ThomasNelson.com.

Unless otherwise noted, Scripture quotations are taken from the NEW AMERICAN STANDARD BIBLE®. © The Lockman Foundation 1960, 1962, 1963, 1968, 1971, 1972, 1973, 1975, 1977, 1995. Used by permission.

Library of Congress Cataloging-in-Publication Data

Stanley, Charles F.
    Stuck in reverse : how to let God change your direction / Charles Stanley.
        p. cm.
    Summary: "Helps readers learn how to live in the hope, meaning, and satisfaction God has for them"—Provided by publisher.
    ISBN: 978-1-4002-0094-8 (tradepaper)
    1. Change—Religious aspects—Christianity. I. Title.
BV4509.5.S75 2008
248.4—dc22
                                                    2007041011

Printed in the United States of America
08 07 06 05 RRD 5 4 3 2 1

*I do not regard myself as having laid hold of it yet;
but one thing I do: forgetting what lies behind
and reaching forward to what lies ahead,
I press on toward the goal for the prize
of the upward call of God in Christ Jesus.*

Philippians 3:13–14

CONTENTS

God Will Change Your Direction

Most of us know what it feels like to be lost while driving in an unfamiliar city or neighborhood. One moment we are traveling along without any problem. Then suddenly we are fighting sinking feelings that result from having taken a wrong turn. No matter how hard we try to dismiss the hounding thoughts, the reality cannot be denied. We are on the wrong road, and we are headed in the opposite direction from where we need to be. If we continue, we will be even farther off course. At this point we have to stop and double-check our map so we can figure out how to turn around and get going in the right direction.

We can have the same experience as we travel the road of life. If you feel as though you are lost or you have been traveling for some time in reverse, I want to assure you that

God can change your direction. However, you must be willing to listen for His voice and obey His call. No matter how difficult the challenge may seem or how dark your sin appears, God loves you and He wants to guide you to a place of hope and restoration.

At one of the toughest junctures of his life, the apostle Paul wrote, "I do not regard myself as having laid hold of [God's goal] yet; but one thing I do: forgetting what lies behind and reaching forward to what lies ahead, I press on toward the goal for the prize of the upward call of God in Christ Jesus" (Phil. 3:13–14).

Paul's heart was not set on worldly passions or pleasing a group of people. It was set only on one thing—living for Jesus Christ. He wanted to know the Savior. He refused to allow negative feelings to weigh him down or prevent him from experiencing God's love and grace. He also resisted the pull of this world and its many snares, which were set to spiritually bind and cripple him.

There are many people who are emotionally, mentally, and physically stuck because they have believed Satan's age-old lie that says we do not need God. Adam and Eve fell into the same trap. They doubted the Lord's goodness and faithfulness. In doing so, they never experienced the peace and joy that come from having an intimate relationship with the Savior.

When you realize you have taken a wrong turn in life, you need to stop and pray. God knows exactly where you are and what it will take to lead you home. He is not embarrassed by your sin or shortcomings, and He openly proclaims His love for you. Confessing your sin to Him opens up a line of communication between you and the Savior that nothing can break.

Second, ask Him to forgive you. God will never give up on you. His overarching plan is for you to come to know Him as your Savior and Lord. This is His ultimate will. However, He also has many plans and desires for your life—all of which are incredible and full of His hope for the future. One wrong decision or even a series of failures cannot diminish His love for you. He meets you right where you are and gives you a bright new future.

Third, ask God to motivate you so that you will begin to go forward by following His road map instead of the selfish desires of your heart. He answers prayer, and He is always willing to forgive and restore. Any discipline He allows to touch your life is designed with a loving purpose to teach you how to follow and obey Him. The world may offer temporary happiness, but only God gives abundant joy that lasts an eternity.

People who realize they are traveling in reverse usually respond in one of two ways: either they turn and walk toward the Lord, or they ignore His call and continue traveling in misery and sorrow. You do not have to travel away from God any longer. Right now you can turn and walk toward the one Person who loves you just the way you are. The moment you acknowledge that you have taken the wrong route and that you want your life to change, God moves mightily on your behalf (Isa. 30:18–19).

In Joel, He tells us, "I will make up to you for the years that the swarming locust has eaten" (2:25). You may have drifted in your devotion to the Lord, but He is waiting for you to return to Him. Or perhaps you have never made a commitment to love and obey Him. My prayer is that this book will be used in your life to encourage you to follow the Savior and begin to spend time with Him in prayer and worship.

If you will allow God to work, He will restore all that has been lost. It may not be exactly the same, but whatever He gives, it will be more than enough to meet every need you have, to the point of overflowing.

Charles F. Stanley

CHAPTER ONE

How Did You Get Here?

It was a beautiful day—the kind that seemed perfect in every way. The weather was fantastic, the scenery was beautiful, and the temperature was just right. I had traveled to Oregon on a photography trip. A few days into the venture, I found myself driving on a road built alongside a rambling river with numerous waterfalls. I had gotten up before dawn to have the correct light for the photographs I wanted to take. However, after stopping beside the river I realized something was not right. The lighting was wrong, and I knew it would be later in the day before it would be exactly what I needed for my photographs.

Since I had plenty of time, I decided to look over the map to see what other points of interest were close by. I remembered that Mount Hood was only a few miles away, but could I drive there before the sun was too high? Early in the morning and late in the evening are some of the best times to photograph. This is when the colors are the richest and most inviting.

As I suspected, Mount Hood was only a short drive away. However, I needed to get away from the cloister of the river and find a road that would lead me to an area that overlooked the mountain. I also noticed on the map that there was a small lake near the mountain, and I began to imagine taking a photograph of the mountain's reflection in the small glasslike lake. The scene would be quiet, thought provoking, and most of all, one that would portray the glory of God's majesty. So I started my car and headed in Mount Hood's direction.

I continued along the road until—just as I had imagined—a small mirrorlike lake appeared in the distance. Looming in the background was the image of Mount Hood in all its inescapable wonder. I pulled the car over and parked in a place where I could unload my equipment and set it up. After taking several photos, I walked back to the car, climbed in, and thought that since the lighting had changed, I would return to the river and finish photographing the stream that had appeared so relaxing earlier.

At that moment, a thought passed through my mind

urging me to check the gas gauge. To my shock, it was close to empty. I had been completely absorbed in what I was doing—photographing the beautiful scenery and enjoying my surroundings—but now my mind raced to retrace the route I had taken an hour earlier. Suddenly I remembered that I had not passed a gas station. Quickly I grabbed the map and confirmed what I already had thought: the nearest town was miles away, and I did not have enough gas to get there.

It appeared I was stuck!

God Always Has the Answer We Need

Many people spend a great part of their lives living out over and over again what I have just described. They start out living for the Lord—walking step-by-step beside Him—and then suddenly they are off running in a different direction, never thinking about the consequences of their actions or their choices.

I was miles away from where I was staying, and I realized I needed help. Daylight in a mountainous area can disappear quickly, and I did not want to spend the night in the shadow of Mount Hood.

What do you do when you realize you are in the wrong place—stuck in reverse when you should be moving forward? Many people panic or simply collapse and give up.

But God never wants us to do that. His desire is for us to learn to trust Him at all times in all kinds of situations.

Immediately I prayed, "Lord, You know my circumstances. You know how far the next gas station is from where I am located. You are totally in control, and I am asking You to send me the help I need." In faith, I turned the key over in the ignition. However, before I could put the car into drive, I heard something that sounded like a very large truck coming in my direction. To my amazement, it was a power company truck. The man driving it pulled into a space right in front of my car. He got out and climbed a nearby utility pole, adjusted something, and came back down.

I got out of the car and waited for him, believing that he was the answer to my prayer. Then I walked over to him and asked, "Can you tell me where I can find a gas station?"

The man smiled and said, "Sure!" He pointed down the road and said, "Go up this road about another quarter of a mile, turn left, and you will see one on your right." Then he said good-bye, climbed back into his truck, and drove away.

I got back into my car and thought about what I would have done had he not stopped. More than likely, I would have driven back the way I had come and run out of gas. When we do realize we are in trouble, we want to rush back to a point of safety. God, however, knows the beginning and the end. He knows the right route for us to travel from one point to another. The shortest and safest way for us to travel is the route He chooses. God has always provided exactly what I needed—when I needed it.

The Right Direction

The one thing we must remember is that God is waiting for us to call out to Him so He can work in our circumstances and straighten out the problems we are facing. When our hearts are turned toward Him in sincere devotion, He will speak to us and show us the right way to go every time. After filling my gas tank, I headed back in the direction of the river I had driven beside earlier and took some terrific photographs.

You may feel as though you are totally out of fuel. Or you may feel as though you are traveling backward. Instead of going forward in life, you are either stuck on the side of the road or in reverse. What do you do? How do you pick up the pieces of your shattered life after suffering a deep blow of discouragement? Is there a way out of the storm that seems to have broken over your life? The answer is yes. God knows the surest route for you to take to the closest fueling station.

In fact, the distance is usually no more than about twelve to sixteen inches or whatever distance it is for you to fall to your knees in prayer. When we cry out to God, He always listens and never fails to answer.

You may have spent many years living out what you thought were your dreams. What you have found is that they are broken dreams and you are far, far from home. Through Jesus Christ, there is hope for the future, love enough to last an eternity, and grace enough to cover every sin you have committed. Even if you feel as though your gas tank is completely empty and there is no hope for your future, God still has a plan, and because He loves you with an everlasting love, there is always hope through Jesus Christ. He is the source of your every need.

CHAPTER TWO

Making a Wrong Turn

The teenager driving his parent's car began to think about what it would feel like to be able to shift gears. Even though the car had an automatic transmission, he imagined shifting into first gear, then into second, and up into third. Because the gearshift was located on the floorboard between the two front seats, the temptation to continue his game seemed all the more fun.

With the radio turned up, he reached down, placed his hand on the gearshift, and gave it another quick pull. However, this time instead of dropping into a lower forward gear, his hand slipped and he accidentally put the car into reverse.

Even before he could step on the brake, he knew there was a major problem. The lights across the dashboard lit up, and just as the car came to a screeching halt, a loud grinding noise emerged from the area where the transmission was located. As he stepped out of the automobile, the only thing that appeared to be working was the bell-like noise telling him the key was still in the ignition!

Not a Laughing Matter

Some of us may smile and shake our heads in disbelief over a story like this one. However, for some, the scenario is all too real. Traveling through life, they barely give God a second thought. Their lives are focused on achieving the things they believe will give them a sense of self-importance, status, and recognition. They feel as though they are moving forward; that is, until they decide to shift into a higher gear and actually drop back into reverse. They find that they can barely make it through a day without fighting thoughts of failure. "What went wrong?" a young man once asked me. "How did life turn out like this? I was sure I was going to be promoted. Why did God allow me to lose my job?"

Before we go any further, I want to assure you that no matter what your circumstances, God is aware of your greatest need. He knows the disappointment you are facing. He also knows the frustration that could be headed your way if you fail to set the focus of your heart on Him instead of the things of this world.

The prophet Isaiah writes, "The LORD will continually guide you, and satisfy your desire in scorched places, and give strength to your bones; and you will be like a watered garden, and like a spring of water whose waters do not fail" (58:11). God also knows your potential, and if you will allow Him, He will show you how to live each day in the light of His success and victory over all defeat. It does not matter what you are facing—financial ruin, scattered dreams, a broken relationship, or some other serious disappointment.

The truth is we do not have to go far to find people struggling to gain some sense of hope for the future. Over the past few years, many have faced disappointments professionally, as well as heartaches in the home. No one enjoys traveling in reverse, and no one has to live this way.

If you feel as though you have downshifted from drive into another gear, you can turn your life around—go in a different direction and begin to live again. While there may be consequences to some decisions you have made in the past, you can start where you are right now and live the life you were created to live. However, you must be willing to open up your heart to God and the plans He has for you. This means being willing to trust Him, to allow Him to lead you each day, and then to give yourself to Him knowing He will take care of all that concerns you.

When We Overlook God

On the other hand, many people, without thinking, shift their lives into overdrive. They never consider the Lord or what good plans He has for them. They are speeding through life never stopping to consider His eternal love and concern until something terrible happens. Then, alone with their fears, they wonder how they will ever be able to live life fully. There is a way, but it is God's way and not the way of this world.

Others have fallen behind because they are trapped in situations they cannot change. God understands their plight. He knows when the burdens we are carrying become too heavy. This is the reason He promises to bear them for us (Ps. 68:19).

Instead of looking through the windshield of hope and possibility and moving forward, far too many people have purposefully placed their lives in reverse and are moving backward. They have believed lies—words spoken that are simply not true, statements that have lowered their self-esteem or changed the focus of their hearts so that they now feel as though they will never move past this point in time. None of this is true. They notice their peers and friends moving forward, but they fail to believe in God's ability to change the direction of their own lives. Therefore, they become stuck in feelings of defeat and disillusionment. If either of these words describes your life, then I want to assure you that you are not alone.

All of us have struggled with feelings of self-doubt and discouragement. Even the godly men and women in God's Word battled many fears and temptations. However, they learned that resignation and disobedience only lead to further disappointment and defeat. God has not designed you for failure. He created you for success—not success from the world's perspective, but success His way—which glorifies and honors Him and also brings many blessings.

A Promise of Hope

Abraham, the one person who is called God's friend in the Bible, would understand our confusing circumstances (2 Chron. 20:7; Isa. 41:8; James 2:23). He grew up in a pagan culture—one that involved the worship of false gods—which is similar to our culture that worships a long list of idols. We usually do not think of his life as being stuck in reverse because he is the patriarch of God's people. However, he did not begin to move forward until the Lord called to him and brought him into a relationship with Him, teaching him how to worship the one true living God. And when God called, Abraham obeyed by answering His call. He was seventy-five years old when God instructed him to leave his home and go to the land the Lord had planned to give him.

Age is not a factor in God's plan. Abraham's obedience was the key that unlocked God's promise, and the same is true for you. When Abraham took his wife, Sarah, and left his home to go to Canaan, he began a journey of faith and obedience that continued for the rest of his life. In fact, by reading the story of his life in Genesis, you can learn exactly what godly obedience looks like.

Over the years, there were times when Abraham took a wrong turn, made a bad decision, or fell into disobedience. However, God did not abandon him or remove His love from him. The Lord is forever faithful. His care and concern for Abraham never shifted or changed, and the same is true for you and me. Whenever we get off track, take a wrong turn, or shift into the wrong gear, God is patient with us. He disciplines us to get us back on track and to a point of restoration in our relationship with Him.

The principles I share with you in this book are designed to help you shift out of reverse and back into drive and into God's plan for your life. If this is to happen, you must be willing to submit your life to Him and take the following steps:

Admit your need for a change. God saw something within Abraham's heart that drew Him close. God had called Abraham to be the father of an entire nation; however, He also recognized that Abraham had a limited free will. This means he could choose to heed the call of God or not. The same is true of our lives. We can do what God instructs us to do, or we can stop and be captured by sin, complacency, and feelings of hopelessness. When we are stuck—boxed in on all sides—and feel as though there is no place left to turn, we quickly become willing to call out to God. Abraham did not wait for life to become difficult before he did what the Lord had created him to do. He responded to God's call with obedience.

Many people fail to realize God has designed them for a specific purpose. He does not call everyone into ministry, but He certainly calls each one of us to worship and live our lives for Him. He has plans and goals He longs for us to reach so that we might experience His blessings as we glorify Him. When we live our lives for Him, we gain a new sense of security, freedom, and hope unlike anything we have known. We also shift into a different gear. This time, though, it is a shift out of reverse and into an eternal forward drive.

There is always a sense of emptiness within the heart of a person who does not know the Savior. But Jesus tells us in John 8:32 that God's truth—the knowledge of His expressed will and purpose for our lives—sets us free from the bondage of sin, sorrow, defeat, anger, and anything else that causes us to live life in reverse. The truth He is talking about in this Scripture is not a worldly truth based on a philosophical argument. It is a truth based on the Word of God—written out for us as a reflection of His unconditional love and grace.

It is the gift of His salvation for all who turn to Him seeking forgiveness for their sins and restoration for their weary souls. When we come to Him, He opens His arms of love and gathers us close. No one is ever turned away. The power of sin is broken, and the bondage we once felt is released. Driving in reverse becomes a thing of the past.

Take a step of faith. Until you give your life and heart to Jesus Christ, you will spend most of your life running in reverse. From the world's point of view, there may seem to be many successful men and women. However, at the end of their lives, they do not have anything of eternal value to show for their efforts.

Their hope was in their money, material possessions, and lifestyle. People can be very successful, but until they know Jesus Christ as Savior and loving Lord, they will be rushing around and feeling anxiety and stress over how to sustain the success they have achieved.

There was something about meeting God and hearing His voice that changed Abraham's life view. One day he was going in one direction, but after God spoke to him, he changed course—just that quickly. There were no questions asked. He just obeyed God by faith. Many times we want to know everything there is to know about a situation before we take the first step. The danger, however, comes when we fail to keep our hearts open and sensitive to the voice of God.

Questioning, doubting, and guessing what could or could not happen in the future erode one's faith. Remember when Jesus told the disciples to allow the children to come to Him (Matt. 19:14)? Children are open to learning and they trust easily. The innocence of a child is powerful because generally it has not been shaped or molded by the heartache, greed, and disappointments of this world. The principle that Jesus was teaching His disciples was a very simple one: all of us need to come to Him as children who long to experience and know the depth of His love and goodness (Mark 10:14). Those who come to the Savior with a childlike heart and sense of trust spend very little time driving in reverse.

Listen for His guidance. For years I have used one word that has become somewhat of a trademark. It is the word *listen.* Usually, when I am preaching and come to a very important part of the sermon, I will say, "Listen to what God is telling us in this Scripture." It is something that comes very naturally because I want people to hear and understand God's truth. I have noticed that whenever I say this, people listen intently. My desire is for them to hear what God has to say about their circumstances.

In this same way, the Holy Spirit urges us to listen for God's voice as we read His Word. We may not actually hear the word *listen*, but we get a sense that this is what God is saying to us. "Listen and I will guide you."

In Psalm 32:8, God says, "I will instruct you and teach you in the way which you should go; I will counsel you with My eye upon you."

He is instructing you to listen to His words so that you will gain understanding for your life. It is as though He is saying, "Listen to Me and you will have a sense of peace unlike anything this world has to offer. You also will have the hope and security that you have longed to achieve. Listen and you will know Me. I will guide you and you will not be afraid."

Are you listening for the voice of God? Most people have a hard time doing this because of the activity and noise that are in their lives—noise that comes from worrying and chasing thoughts of doubt as well as visions of grandeur.

The noise of the world's chants calling us to abandon our faith and live only for ourselves floods our minds with thoughts that are totally opposed to God's will and plan for us. In order to hear His voice, there will be times when we must be willing to put our lives in park and be still before Him in prayer and faith. You may think, *I don't have time to wait or to stop.* The truth is, when your life is suddenly slammed into reverse and the transmission begins to grind under the pressure that you have placed on it, you will want to stop and listen. When you do, He will speak to your heart just as He spoke to Abraham.

Move forward when He tells you to go. The Bible tells us that when God called to Abraham, he "went forth as the LORD had spoken to him" (Gen. 12:4). In other words, he did not hesitate. He did not wait for God to tell him what to do a second time, and he did not wait until everything was revealed to him concerning the future. In fact, the author of Hebrews writes, "By faith Abraham, when he was called, obeyed by going out to a place which he was to receive for an inheritance; and he went out, not knowing where he was going" (11:8).

The reason many people become stuck in reverse and actually end up going in the opposite direction from the one God planned for them is because they fail to step out and go forward by faith. This does not mean rushing blindly into a situation, but it does mean being sensitive to the open door that God places before you. Had Abraham refused to do this, he would have taken a detour around God's will and blessing.

Be committed to waiting for His timing. Anytime we say yes to God, we also must be willing to wait for His perfect timing. Moses made things more difficult by striking out on his own before God had given him clear direction. He ended up killing an Egyptian and could have jeopardized God's mission to deliver the nation of Israel. But God is sovereign and He knew the wrong turn Moses would take. Years later, after Moses had learned to listen for God's voice, he returned to Egypt and led the nation of Israel out of captivity and to the doorstep of the Promised Land.

God may ask you to wait for a season of time before He reveals His plans for your life. During times of godly waiting, you are not stuck in reverse. In fact, from God's perspective you are moving forward because you are waiting in faith for His next instruction. Most of God's greatest saints have gone through times when they have had to wait. Often the Lord only gives us light enough for the step that we will take today. This is why the psalmist writes, "Your word is a lamp to my feet and a light to my path" (119:105).

In times of waiting, be committed to being patient, knowing that you will receive God's very best as you look to Him for guidance. Also, use this time to read and study

His Word. You may feel as though you are in a holding pattern—going nowhere—but God is preparing you for a greater work—one that will be glorifying to Him and one that will position you for His blessings.

There is a basic truth to shifting your life out of reverse and into a forward gear, and it is this: no matter what your circumstances are or what you have done in the past, God loves you with an everlasting love, and He will make your life count for something wonderful, if you will place your trust in Him.

CHAPTER THREE

Why We Hesitate

Hesitate while swinging at a baseball and you will miss it completely. Take a moment to think about how you will finish a 10k run once it has started, and chances are you will lose the race. Hesitation signals an unsure attitude, doubt, and sometimes a lack of faith and belief in what you are doing. While there are times when God wants us to wait for His answer to our prayers, there are other times when He instructs us to move forward in boldness, believing that He will provide exactly what He has promised.

Have you ever hesitated and missed an important opportunity? Most of us have. When this happens, the questions that need to be answered are ones like these: "Do I believe God has created me for a purpose?" "Am I sure that He has a plan for my life and that He is willing to give me the wisdom and strength I need to reach my full potential?" If your answer is yes, then there is no way you will continue living life running in reverse. However, if you said no and hesitated, then you will feel the stress that comes from being held captive to thoughts of doubt and insecurity. Never allow these to hold you back because God has placed His seal of ownership on your life. You are His, and your life contains all you need to reach the goals He sets for you.

God's Plan for You

Each one of us will go through times when we wonder if what we are doing really counts or makes a difference. We may feel disappointed when there is suddenly a shift in the course we have chosen to follow. Feelings of frustration and low self-esteem only fuel our inability to move forward, and we can end up languishing in thoughts of failure over goals not reached. Remember these truths:

- God wants you to move forward each day.
- Even if you cannot see tangible progress, He can.
- He is at work in our lives on all fronts, preparing us for something greater and better.
- When we trust Him, He moves on our behalf.

God has given each one of us a basic promise to cling to whenever we are tempted to doubt His goodness. It is Jeremiah 29:11: "'I know the plans that I have for you,' declares the LORD, 'plans for welfare and not for calamity to give you a future and a hope.'"

In these few words, God has given us a powerful promise. However, He also has revealed a life-changing view of Himself. He tells us, "I know the plans that I have." Think about these words for a moment in light of where you are today and what you would like to achieve. Some may say, "I'm right on track. Thank You, Lord." Many more would have to confess that they wish they could know what God knows about their future. Is there hope? Does He really care? The answer is yes!

You may be thinking, *I've tried and nothing seems to work. Why try again and risk being disappointed? At least I can stay where I am and feel comfortable.* Few people enjoy watching others move forward in life while they remain behind the starting gate. Secretly and deep down inside, each one of us wants to achieve something wonderful in life. This is perfectly normal.

God created you with a plan in mind. It is not a plan of failure. It is one of success and blessing. However, many who teach God's Word have distorted this truth by encouraging people to make worldly success their goal. Success from God's perspective is a continuing achievement of becoming the person He wants you to become. It also includes accomplishing the goals He helps you set for your life. The word *failure* is not in His vocabulary—neither are any words that produce condemnation or hopelessness.

Success in God's eyes does not necessarily mean becoming president of a company or acquiring great wealth. However, it does mean doing what He has created us to do—using our gifts and talents to fulfill our greatest potential, which always glorifies God in the process. But when we allow the focus of our hearts to be turned away from the course that we have been given to travel, we risk suffering a great defeat.

God instructed the nation of Israel to go into the Promised Land and take it as their inheritance. But they balked at the idea and hesitated to do what God had commanded them to do. Why does the Lord allow us to face a challenge that seems beyond anything we could accomplish?

The answer is simple. He wants us to learn to depend totally on Him—to listen for His voice and to view Him as our provider for every need we have. If we can figure out a way to reach the goal or complete the task apart from Him, then we will no longer walk by faith but will walk in light of what we can accomplish on our own. For God to be truly glorified in our lives, we must learn to live by faith, trusting Him every step of the way.

An Unforgettable Lesson

Moses never forgot what happened at Kadesh-Barnea (Num. 13:26). Not because this was a place of victory, but because it was a place of extreme frustration and one that ultimately led to Israel's spending forty more years wandering in the wilderness. Kadesh was the name of Israel's encampment in the wilderness of Paran, and it was also a place of emotional defeat for God's people. Moses had sent twelve spies into the land of Canaan. Their mission was simple: go into the land, make a mental note of what they saw, and return to the camp with an update.

The question on the table was not whether the nation should enter the land—this already had been settled by God years earlier through a covenant He had made with Abraham. These men were on a fact-finding mission. They were to return with news concerning the structure of the cities within the land, the nature of the people, and the bounty that was there: was it truly a place that flowed with milk and honey (Num. 13:18–20)?

Whenever God gives us a directive, we need to do what

He is telling us to do based simply on one thing—who is doing the talking. In other words, God had commanded the people to take the land. That should have been the end of the discussion. The size and power of the people should not have been issues. God's command remained the same—claim what I have given you. Go forward!

The spies entered the land, and after forty days, they returned to the camp with a report. However, the news they brought back with them struck fear in the hearts of God's people:

> "We went in to the land where you sent us; and it certainly does flow with milk and honey, and this is its fruit. Nevertheless, the people who live in the land are strong, and the cities are fortified and very large; and moreover, we saw the descendants of Anak there. Amalek is living in the land of the Negev and the Hittites and the Jebusites and the Amorites are living in the hill country, and the Canaanites are living by the sea and by the side of the Jordan.
>
> ". . . We became like grasshoppers in our own sight, and so we were in their sight." (Num. 13:27–29, 33)

By this point, the people were agitated and doubtful they could conquer their enemies. Caleb, a man of faith, quieted the people and said, "We should by all means go up and take possession of it, for we will surely overcome it" (v. 30).

But the people of God allowed fear to capture their hearts. They refused to trust Him and enter the land that had been given to them. As a result of their decision, they spent forty years wandering in the desert—outside the Promised Land.

Instead of going forward by faith, the people hesitated. Their thinking was stuck in reverse. They could not imagine how they could conquer the nations that were already in possession of the land that was rightfully theirs. We will face many challenges in life—some will be enjoyable and others will not. However, no matter how great a challenge may be, if God has led us to a certain point with the promise of leading us on to victory, then we can trust Him to grant His blessing and also to guide us every step of the way.

Following God's Road Map

Years ago God began to make it clear that He was going to use our church in a mighty way. The history of our church reveals a strong desire to take the gospel message to a lost world. However, in the beginning no one could envision how. The first challenge we faced was a need to expand our tape ministry. We had started with a simple idea of making our Sunday worship services available on cassette tape. Soon we realized that we had more requests than we could answer. We purchased a few pieces of new equipment and never had an opportunity to look back.

This is how the ministry of In Touch began—with one simple step of obedience and faith. We were on television as well as the radio. Soon there was a need for new cameras in order to upgrade our television program. The need was mentioned to the congregation, and they responded by giving enough money to purchase what was needed.

Our church was growing. College students and youth packed our Sunday school facilities every week, and we knew we would have to expand, but how? At the time, we were in a location that was landlocked—meaning that the church was surrounded by businesses and other worship facilities. The only course of action we had was to pray for property to become available for purchase in the heart of a major city that also was in the middle of growth and expansion.

We prayed, and God opened one door after another. Each time we trusted Him for the amount of money needed to close the deal. During one major purchase of a piece of property that had been used as a nightclub, we literally stepped out on faith and trusted Him to set up the circumstances for the building and the land to be sold because the owners were firm in their decision not to sell to us.

In my heart, I knew God was working. He had led us this far, giving us one promise after another. Therefore I knew He would provide for our needs. After rereading the story of Joshua entering the Promised Land and especially conquering the city of Jericho, I asked the pastoral staff to join me one morning in the back parking lot. I described to them what we were going to do and watched as a look of boldness and faith appeared on their faces.

I had never done anything like this before, but we walked over to the building and property that we wanted to purchase and began walking around it. Everyone was instructed to say nothing. They were told to just walk and pray, believing God would find a way to give us this building for our youth.

Sure enough, a few weeks later, the owner of the property called saying that he was ready to sell to us. The point of this story is to underscore the importance of obedience and faith in an omnipotent God. We think that obeying God means doing the right thing, much like a child would obey his or her mother when she says, "Don't slam the door," "Sit up straight in your chair," or "Be sure you are home before 11:00 p.m."

However, obedience to God goes far beyond the simple requests of a parent or employer. He sees far beyond the limits of our present circumstances. He knows that if we have learned to obey Him in the simple times, then He can trust us with great challenges.

God did not turn to the nation of Israel one morning with the command to go in and take away land that was owned by their enemies. He had led them out of Egyptian bondage and coached them through times of difficulty so they would know that He was God and would lead them into the Promised Land.

This was the point of the Exodus, not just to bring freedom to His people, but also to bring them into a place of blessing—the Promised Land. However, the first time Israel approached the land they did not claim it, nor did they place their trust in God, but instead they considered the situation in light of their own ability.

Never calculate the faithfulness of God by what you think you can do. People who end up traveling through life in reverse or being stuck in a lower gear have never learned to lift their eyes to the infinite ability of God. There is nothing too difficult for Him and nothing too hard for us when our lives are committed to following Him (Jer. 32:17).

It was too late when Israel realized they had refused to take the land God had given them. They fell into rebellion, and if Moses and Aaron had not stepped in and prayed for them, God would have destroyed the people. His anger subsided, but He made it clear that no one from the present generation would enter into His promised blessing. It would be another generation—the children of these men and women—who would inherit the land.

When the people heard this, they "mourned greatly" (Num. 14:39). They also decided that they would go into the land after all and claim it as theirs. However, God was not with them. For the moment, the window of opportunity had closed. When they tried to conquer the nations residing in the Promised Land, they were soundly defeated.

Notice, however, that God's plan remained firmly in place. He would take His people into the land, but it would be at a later date, and no one from the Exodus generation except for Joshua and Caleb would be able to claim what God had given His people. Only the children of that generation would go into the land. Often when we fail to do what God has instructed us to do, we find ourselves having to wait in order to have another opportunity to experience His blessing.

Sadly, there are times when we will not be given another chance. Yet God does not leave us in a backward state. As we learn to obey Him, He provides other opportunities for blessing and hope. In times of failure, the most important lesson we can learn is to trust Him for the future.

You may have been given a great opportunity for growth in your vocation or in your personal life. However, feelings of fear and a low self-esteem have tripped you up and you have allowed them to hold you back. Instead of making progress in your spiritual and professional life, you have gone backward. You can stop the downward or backward spiral by telling God:

- You want His best for your life.
- You want to grow even though you feel inadequate.
- You are willing to trust Him and obey Him fully.

He knows your weaknesses, and He is committed to teaching you how to walk in the light of His strength and power each day. It is a walk of faith, and it is foundational to everything else you do with and for God.

David was anointed king at a very young age, but he spent years being prepared to rule the nation of Israel. There were times when it seemed as though his life was spiraling out of control. These were the very times he called out to God for help and understanding, and you can learn to do the same.

True wisdom and strength for every challenge we face come from God—not from human reasoning or knowledge. We can learn a great deal in this life, but if we are not basing what we know on the unshakable knowledge of Christ, then any success we experience will be either short-lived or empty. It is the supernatural power of God living within us through the presence of the Holy Spirit that gives us the understanding we need to follow and serve Him. He is the One who prepares us for a good work—a work that will stand the test of time and lead others into a saving knowledge of God's Son—the Lord Jesus Christ.

David writes, "Make me know Your ways, O LORD; teach me Your paths. Lead me in Your truth and teach me, for You are the God of my salvation; for You I wait all the day. Remember, O LORD, Your compassion and Your lovingkindnesses, for they have been from of old. Do not remember the sins of my youth or my transgressions; according to Your lovingkindness remember me, for Your goodness' sake, O LORD" (Ps. 25:4–7).

When we are waiting in obedience to the Lord, we are not stuck in reverse because waiting involves an active, dynamic faith. David learned this at a young age. God allowed him to face many challenges that could have threatened his faith, but none did.

Abraham's obedience seemed immediate. However, just like us, he had to learn to walk with God, to trust Him in times of great stress, and also to be willing to wait forever if necessary to receive the blessing God had planned for him.

Neither David nor Abraham lived lives that were stuck in reverse because they were committed to gaining the promises of God. While they did not have the complete picture of God's future provision, they trusted and obeyed, and this made all the difference in their lives.

Are you trusting God for your circumstances? Do you believe that He is working behind the scenes in order to put everything together for your good pleasure and His glory? When you live in God's blessings, He is glorified and others are drawn to Him. This does not necessarily mean that you will be wealthy and have many possessions. His greatest blessings—peace, joy, and love—do not rust or fade with time (Matt. 6:19–20).

The Brink of a Blessing

One of the first things God looks for in the life of a believer is faithfulness. If this is present in the hearts of those who follow Him, then obedience will be there, too, and this is the doorway to personal growth and success.

There is no way our church congregation could have known the many ways God would use us to carry the message of His truth around the world. One step of faith and obedience led to another until we were at a crossroads—a place where we had to claim the promise of God as being ours and move in to take the land He had given us.

Another piece of property became available, but this time the price tag was much higher and would require an even greater sacrifice. We planned to use the property for the offices of In Touch—our media ministry that had outgrown all of the facilities that we had set aside for it. In a unanimous vote, we chose to buy the property that encompassed several blocks of land in downtown Atlanta. The most amazing part of this journey was how the people responded to the obvious leading of the Lord. They chose to trust God for the funds we needed and not to borrow a single penny.

We had time to raise the money, but God does not keep a calendar the way we do. He never does business solely by human standards. He uses human institutions as avenues for Him to display His wondrous power. Therefore I did not think it was unusual to see the deadline drawing near and not have the full amount needed for the purchase. Over the weeks leading up to this moment, people had given sacrificially. Some had offered personal items such as wedding rings, homes, and other things that had great sentimental value.

I never once asked anyone to give anything. All I asked was that they would be obedient to God. If purchasing this property was a part of His will for our church, He would provide the money we needed. As word spread about what we were doing, we noticed that people not even connected with our church were giving to our building fund.

I realized if we did not seize this opportunity, we could risk following the same line of thinking Israel took at Kadesh-Barnea. Failing to trust Him now would mean failure and the possible loss of a blessing. By blessing, I mean our opportunity to be a channel of hope and truth to a lost and dying world. None of us wanted this to happen.

Again, God had not given us a complete road map for the future, but He had provided enough spiritual light for us to take the next step. Many times this is all we are given—light for the next step in front of us. We take it and then there is light given for the next one and the one after that. It all begins with faith in a loving God who has promised never to guide us in the wrong direction.

However, there was something restless within my heart. Did I fully believe God would provide all the money? On Saturday afternoon before I preached on Sunday—the day before we were scheduled to meet with the bank and pay for the property—I went for a walk alone. Suddenly I sensed God speaking to me. His words came from the book of Isaiah and were very pointed. "Who is among you that fears the LORD, that obeys the voice of His servant, that walks in darkness and has no light? Let him trust in the name of the LORD and rely on his God. Behold, all you who kindle a fire, who encircle yourselves with firebrands, walk in the light of your fire and among the brands you have set ablaze. This you will have from My hand: you will lie down in torment" (50:10–11). This was an awesome promise, but at the same time, it was a stiff warning from God.

If we continued to trust Him for the provision, He would prove faithful. Up to that point, I had quietly wondered what to do should the deadline come and go and we were short of money. Would it be feasible to borrow what was needed to close the deal? Suddenly I knew if we decided to turn to a financial institution to help us with the purchase, we would risk missing God's best.

The Lord knew my heart. He also understood I only wanted what He desired for our church and its future. He was in total control of the situation, and I believed He would faithfully provide what we needed. Therefore I determined that we would not even entertain the thought of borrowing one single copper penny. And we did not. The next morning I got up to preach with a sense of freshness and hope. All my questions had been answered. There was no sense of burden because I had given everything to Him.

The title of my message that morning was "On the Brink of a Blessing," and this is where we stood—on the edge of our Promised Land—and we were determined to enter. And enter we did. In fact, we went to the meeting the next day, right on time and with just enough money to pay for this valuable piece of property in cash.

Lives were changed in the process of this one event. I will never forget how God perfectly provided for a need that led our church through an open door and paved the way for His Word to be preached in every corner of the world. What does this mean for you, as a child of God?

He has a plan for your life. Therefore you do not have to spend your life stuck in reverse. Jeremiah 29:11 is a verse you can claim concerning your future. No matter what has happened in the past, God will meet you right where you are, and He will develop His plan within your life when you submit your heart to Him. Submission is an essential step in receiving God's promises and blessings.

One of the reasons people fail to trust God and seek His plan for their lives is because they become too wrapped up in their own desires, thoughts, and dreams for the future. The focus of their lives is not set on God and doing His will. It is set on fulfilling their own desires— desires that frequently are not in keeping with His plan and purpose.

The nation of Israel was too concerned about their personal lives and not enough about God's work in their hearts and circumstances. They failed to believe Him for the victory. "We went in to the land where you sent us; and it certainly does flow with milk and honey, and this is its fruit. Nevertheless, the people who live in the land are strong, and the cities are fortified and very large" (Num. 13:27–28).

Having the wrong perspective can lead to defeat. Instead of focusing on the One who is above all things and omnipotent in power, they allowed their hearts to be ruled by feelings of doubt, which led them to back away from the Promised Land.

Sin also can prevent us from experiencing God's best. It was the sin of rebellion against God that barred Israel from receiving His best. But after spending forty years in the wilderness, the next time God instructed them to go in and take what He had given them, they did exactly what He commanded them to do (Josh. 1–4).

When we fail to obey God, we miss His blessing. However, while there are times when we may not be given a second opportunity, God never gives up on us. If we are faithful in our obedience to Him and devote ourselves to knowing Him, He will change our hearts and bring us into a place of blessing and hope.

You can trust Him to do exceedingly above all you can think or imagine. We have a limited view of God's goodness. Though we have been given all we need to see the love of the Father clearly through the life and death of His Son on Calvary's cross, we often only believe what we can see. A bill comes due, and because we have suffered a job loss, we are tempted to feel panicked. The natural questions to ask are "How will I pay this?" and "What will I do?"

However, the right thing to do is to pray, "God, show me how You want me to handle this. Help me to know what to do so that all my bills are paid. You know my circumstance perfectly. Teach me to be a good steward of the funds You have given me for this time in my life and forever. I'm trusting You to provide for all my needs according to Your Word in Philippians 4:19."

Eyes of faith have the ability to see beyond the immediate circumstances to the more than adequate provision of God. Learn to pray and lay out your need before Him. Trust Him and you will see that He will faithfully provide what you need on time, every time.

You do not have to struggle through the circumstances of life because He will guide you every step of the way. One of my favorite verses is found in the book of Proverbs: "Trust in the LORD with all your heart and do not lean on your own understanding. In all your ways acknowledge Him, and He will make your paths straight" (3:5–6).

Think of the emotional, mental, and physical energy you could save or redirect in the right direction by trusting

God and not following what seems right from your perspective. There will be times when God immediately gives you the wisdom you need to make a critical decision. Without a doubt, you know what you should do. When this happens, you can be sure that He has trained you to listen for His guidance and you can step forward. Other times you may not have a clue about what you should be doing. When this happens, wait—be still before Him and ask Him to make His will perfectly clear.

You can enter into the land that He has given to you, but it will require a step of faith along with a heart that longs to know Him better. People who commit their lives to Christ live with a sense of expectation. They are looking for something greater to happen because they know God is at work in their lives. And greater does not mean they are written up in the local newspaper. Greater means the focus of their hearts is set on the Lord. They have learned that He will use them greatly because they have given their lives to Him.

The men and women of the Bible remained faithful amid horrendous circumstances (Heb. 11). They entered the promise of God because their lives were totally devoted to Him. What is your heart's motivation? Are you driven by the winds of society that blow one way today and another way tomorrow? If this is the case, you will find that you are living life in the opposite direction from the one God has called you to live.

How do you set the right course for your life? By learning how to keep the eyes of your heart on Jesus Christ, trusting Him for every need you have, and surrendering your will to Him so that He can make it His and in doing so, fit you—prepare you—for great blessings.

CHAPTER FOUR

Plotting the Right Course

During the early years of growth and expansion, our church congregation adopted several hymns as songs of encouragement and hope. Whenever we sang one of these, the atmosphere surrounding our worship service became charged with the energy of faith.

One particular hymn stands out in my mind as a favorite. I cannot count the number of times we sang this hymn. There were many. However, we never grew tired of singing "Like a River Glorious." Each time we sang the words to this hymn, a balm of encouragement filled our hearts. We were, in fact, learning to fix our minds and hearts on Jehovah our God knowing that when we did, there would be no reason to worry.

Stuck in Reverse

Like a river glorious is God's perfect peace,
Over all victorious in its bright increase;
Perfect, yet it floweth fuller every day
Perfect, yet it groweth deeper all the way.

Stayed upon Jehovah, hearts are fully blest;
Finding, as He promised, perfect peace and rest.

Hidden in the hollow of His blessed hand,
Never foe can follow, never traitor stand;
Not a surge of worry, not a shade of care,
Not a blast of hurry touch the spirit there.

Stayed upon Jehovah, hearts are fully blest;
Finding, as He promised, perfect peace and rest.

Every joy or trial falleth from above,
Traced upon our dial by the Sun of Love;
We may trust him fully all for us to do;
They who trust Him wholly find Him wholly true.

Stayed upon Jehovah, hearts are fully blest;
Finding, as He promised, perfect peace and rest.

When your life is firmly grounded in Christ, temptations may come and challenges may threaten your sense of

peace, but you will not be drawn away from the course God has given you to follow.

Many times, when God gets ready to do something new in our lives, He provides a fresh sense of direction and even leadership. As the nation of Israel prepared to enter the Promised Land, God placed a new man in the leadership role Moses had held for years. Moses did not go with the people into the land but was buried by God just outside its borders. Just as He had been with Moses, He would now be with Joshua, whom He had chosen to lead the people across the Jordan River and into the land He was giving them.

There was no doubt this time: the nation would go forward. No thought of reversing their decision or backing up. They had spent forty years outside of God's blessing, waiting for Him to lead them back to a place where they could demonstrate their devotion and obedience by doing what their fathers had failed to do—believe God for His provision.

Only Be Strong and Very Courageous
The Lord appeared to Joshua saying,

> "Moses My servant is dead; now therefore arise, cross this Jordan, you and all this people, to the land which I am giving to them, to the sons of Israel. Every place on which

the sole of your foot treads, I have given it to you, just as I spoke to Moses. . . . No man will be able to stand before you all the days of your life. Just as I have been with Moses, I will be with you; I will not fail you or forsake you. Be strong and courageous, for you shall give this people possession of the land which I swore to their fathers to give them. Only be strong and very courageous; be careful to do according to all the law which Moses My servant commanded you; do not turn from it to the right or to the left, so that you may have success wherever you go. This book of the law shall not depart from your mouth, but you shall meditate on it day and night, so that you may be careful to do according to all that is written in it; for then you will make your way prosperous, and then you will have success.

"Have I not commanded you? Be strong and courageous! Do not tremble or be dismayed, for the LORD your God is with you wherever you go." (Josh. 1:2–3, 5–9)

Just as He did with Moses and Joshua, God has a purpose in mind for your life. Even before you were born, He had a role for you to fill. No one can do exactly what He wants you to do. You may wonder, *What if I fail to do this? Will God still love me?* Yes. His love for you is not based on what you accomplish. It is unconditional and eternal.

However, when you fail to live the life that He has designed for you to live, you are the one who suffers.

As you read this book, you may feel as though you are an absolute failure, but nothing could be further from the truth. No matter how many times you have walked away from an opportunity thinking that there was no way you could handle the responsibility, God still has a plan in mind for your life. He still wants to encourage you and bring you into a place of blessing where He can use you for His kingdom work on earth. From God's perspective, no one is a loser; no situation is too great for Him to solve.

He knew Joshua would face many challenges. Therefore He mapped out a course that Israel would follow. It was not just a road map like we are accustomed to following. It was also a spiritual map—one that would guide them to a place of victory and success. It is one that we can apply to our lives as well, especially as we seek God's wisdom for the future.

God gave Joshua an extremely important command. He instructed him three times to be "strong and courageous." At one point, the Lord said, "Be strong and very courageous."

The Lord knew Joshua and the people would be tempted to yield to their inner fears. God did not remove their enemies from the land. This was something the people were required to do. He provided the land and the strength they needed to conquer it. However, they would have to drive out their enemies. Those who were against Israel worshiped pagan gods. The Lord knew if the enemies were not removed, then Israel's devotion could become diluted.

People who become stuck in reverse in life face a fearful situation and refuse to go forward. For one reason or another, they begin to believe that they cannot do what God has given them to do. Perhaps they have been given a scholarship to college, a promotion at work, or have entered a new relationship. Instead of thanking God for the opportunity He has provided, they freeze, and this is when the enemy lies to them by telling them that they cannot do the job, accept the responsibility, or enjoy the new friendship. However, the Lord never calls us to do anything without equipping us for the task. While not everyone will become CEO of a major Fortune 500 company, you can achieve all you have been created to be. If that includes being a CEO, then God will provide the ability to do this. In Mark 10:27, we are reminded, "With people it is impossible, but not with God; for all things are possible with God."

Keep Your Mind and Thoughts Set on Christ

The grammar school I attended had a policy: those who passed all the subjects they took could go on to the next grade. However, those who did not do this failed and had to repeat the entire grade. My sixth-grade teacher had a unique way of motivating her students to make better grades. She placed five pictures on a large bulletin board—an airplane, a train, a ship, an automobile, and a field of sheep.

If you made an A on a test, she would write your name under the airplane. Bs were listed under the train, and so it went. Anyone making an F would end up in the field of sheep. There were many days when I entered the classroom to find only my name listed under the field of sheep.

Unfortunately her actions only helped to reinforce the message I was hearing at home from my stepfather. He frequently told me that I would never amount to anything and that I was worthless. These messages landed hard and made a deep impression.

They could have programmed me for failure, weakness, and defeat. However, God had a different message for me, and it is the same one He has for you. In Ephesians 2:10, Paul writes, "For we are His workmanship, created in Christ Jesus for good works, which God prepared beforehand so that we would walk in them." *Workmanship* in the Greek means "a person of notable excellence." Therefore, because of God's love for us, we are people of worth—notable excellence—and dearly loved by Him.

You may not feel excellent, but this is how God views

your life. He has created you as a person of extreme worth, not because of anything you have done, but because of the One your life contains. And if you have accepted His Son as Savior, then your life is hidden in Christ—a place of the highest value, hope, and security.

People who feel inferior will make statements like these: "I'm just dumb," "I can't do it," and "I don't have a degree so I just need to give up." Never give up and never give in. The challenge facing Joshua and the nation of Israel was a huge one, but no one wanted to go back into the desert for another forty years of wandering. No. They decided the next time God gave them an opportunity they would take it. They would enter the land and trust the Lord with the consequences. This is what we need to do each day—obey God and leave the consequences to Him. If you do, you will never be disappointed.

With this in mind, I had to make a decision about life, and that was whether to stay in a mental sheep field or to position myself among the list of those who were flying airplanes. God also placed two people in my life who offered the encouragement I needed to climb up and away from any feelings of defeat that may have been building up inside me. One person God used in my life was a schoolteacher whom I overheard one day saying, "I like Charles." That was it. These three simple words spoken to another teacher were enough to change my outlook. I have never forgotten them. They lifted my heart and motivated me to move forward and not remain stuck in feelings of worthlessness.

The second person was my Sunday school teacher, Craig Stowe. Although he received a newspaper at his home, he often sought me out in the afternoons while I was delivering papers in another neighborhood and bought one from me. It was not long before I realized he did not need another newspaper. Instead, God was using him to encourage me during a difficult time in my life. He always told me that he was praying for me and thinking of me. He was the only man in my life who conveyed that he loved and cared for me.

These two people were God's gifts of encouragement given to a young boy who needed to know he was not a failure and he was not a hopeless cause. Far too many people believe lies that have been carelessly spoken to them out of another person's weakness and insecurity. Never base your life's worth on the critical words of others. Base it on what God has to say about you—you are a person of worth, someone who is loved with an eternal love.

Steps to God's Goal for Your Life

The first principle we need to learn is that we need to trust God's will and plan for our lives. We must be on the same page He is on. If our goals and dreams do not line up with His purpose, then we will struggle and be out of step with His plan. From an earthly standpoint, there are many successful people. However, unless their goal involves the will of God for their lives, they will always have a sense of longing deep within their hearts. It is a longing that cannot be satisfied with material gain or wealth.

Happiness and fulfillment are not found in how much we have or what we do. They are found in being all that God has designed us to be and through achieving the goals and dreams that He has given us. Over the years I have met many people who just do not understand this principle. They strive for significance when they already have been given all they could hope to receive—the unconditional love of God. We do not have to fight to have more. He has given us all of Himself through His Son, the Lord Jesus Christ.

The second principle we can learn from Joshua 1:2–9 is that we never need to be fearful. Wherever we go, God is with us. Whatever we do, He is there to provide the strength, wisdom, talent, and ability to accomplish the task. Even before a need arises, He is aware of it and moves on our behalf to take care of it. There is no need for fear because God loves us and He stands watch over our lives (Ps. 66).

God said to Joshua, "No man will be able to stand

before you all the days of your life. Just as I have been with Moses, I will be with you; I will not fail you or forsake you" (Josh. 1:5). God never leaves us alone to figure out a situation. He is with us—watching over us, leading us, and encouraging us not to give up but to keep going so that we can gain the blessing He has for us.

Living life in reverse means we have made a conscious choice not to go forward because we may be frightened or overwhelmed by our circumstances. However, we are not alone; God is with us, and we can face the future with confidence, believing that He will work everything out for our good and His glory (Rom. 8:28).

Third, we should live a life that is committed to obeying God. Before the people entered the Promised Land, God gave them these instructions:

> "When you have eaten and are satisfied, you shall bless the LORD your God for the good land which He has given you. Beware that you do not forget the LORD your God by not keeping His commandments and His ordinances and His statutes . . . ; otherwise, when you have eaten and are satisfied, and have built good houses and lived in them, and when your herds and your flocks multiply, and your silver and gold multiply, and all that you

have multiplies, then your heart will become proud and you will forget the LORD your God." (Deut. 8:10–14)

God's plan for us is one of prosperity and abundance. You do not have to be wealthy to experience this. In fact, some of the richest people are the ones who have found their wealth and joy in the Lord. The principle that we need to learn is one of dedication. When our hearts and lives are caught up in Him, we will want to obey Him. In fact, obedience will come naturally.

Beyond Feelings

Feelings of inferiority and low self-esteem vanish when our hearts are set on Jesus Christ. But how do we do this, especially when we feel as though life has turned out badly? Is there a way to move our lives out of reverse and into a forward gear? Yes, there is, and there are several ways you can accomplish this.

Ask God to teach you about His personal and intimate love. Often the reason we begin to live life in reverse is because we fail to understand just how much God loves us. We cannot fully grasp His vision for our lives until we take time to get to know Him. When we do, we discover His love for us is greater than anything we have known.

Another important thing to remember is that Satan loves to speak words of condemnation to us. He tries to deceive us by telling us that God is angry with us and does not love us. Nothing could be further from the truth. God's lovingkindness toward you is everlasting (Jer. 31:3). He never withholds His love just because you have disobeyed Him. Certainly sin quenches His Spirit, and you may even sense a distance between you and Him. However, He is not the One who has moved. Temptation and sin draw us away. God, however, is immovable in His loving care for us.

When you accepted Christ as your Savior, God broke the power of sin in your life. You may experience times of temptation, but God does not condemn you. His Son paid the price for your sins on the cross. The apostle Paul writes, "There is now no condemnation for those who are in Christ Jesus" (Rom. 8:1). The freedom that is yours was given to you as a gift of grace from the One who loves you and has nothing but good plans for your life.

Realize that God created you for a purpose, and you are a person of great worth. God has a plan for your life no matter who you are or what you have done in the past. He created you for His glory and also to do good works. It does not matter if you are five or ninety-five; God uses those whose lives are devoted to Him. Sometimes people ask, "If

I give up my personal desires, will I still enjoy what I am doing? Will I be able to achieve my goals?" The greatest joy and sense of peace you will experience is found in doing God's will. In fact, because God is so creative and insightful, you will discover that you have talents and abilities you never knew you had. The moment you submit your life to Him, He goes to work within you—molding and shaping you so that you become all He intends for you to be—which is always much more than you can imagine. Give Him your life, and you will be blessed in more ways than you ever dreamed possible.

Far too often, people mistakenly believe if they have wealth and material possessions, then they will be happy. However, abundant joy is not the result of having material possessions. It is the result of having a personal relationship with the Savior. This is something that cannot be taken away. It does not fade with time or grow old. It is new every morning and abundant in peace and the rich blessings of His fellowship.

Pray that God will give you a deep, abiding love for His Word. One of the surest ways to shift out of reverse and into drive spiritually is to begin spending time in prayer and reading God's Word. The psalmist writes, "Your word I have treasured in my heart, that I may not sin against You" (119:11). When you spend time studying His Word, you begin to build truth into your life. God's Spirit will teach you more about Him. Sin, on the other hand, will become less of a temptation because you will learn that it leads to sorrow, disappointment, brokenness, and feelings of low self-esteem. Always remember: the enemy does not want you to know the effects of sin. He wants you to believe that you will not suffer for your disobedience, but you will. One of the greatest consequences of sin is broken fellowship with the Lord.

Trust God for your future. A lack of sincere trust and faith in God leads to pride as well as feelings of inadequacy. Israel thought they knew what was best. Instead of going forward by faith, they relied on their limited knowledge. Whenever we do this, we run the risk of failure. God knows all things. He sees the beginning and the end. When we pray and ask Him to provide insight into our circumstances, He will. He has the ultimate knowledge we need for every step we take in life. God never forgets His promises. Years later, after Israel had learned a very stiff lesson of faith, they entered the Promised Land. This time fear did not grip their hearts. They plotted the right course by committing themselves to following God's plan and not their own. They were courageous, and they entered into the blessing that the Lord had for them.

Perhaps you are wondering if you can move past this point in time. You have hesitated in fear and doubted

God's goodness. Maybe due to some past hurt, you have found it difficult to trust again. If this is the case, take a step of faith and trust the way that God is calling you to go. He will not only meet you along the path, He will take your hand and guide you to the very place He has planned for you to be. Others who do not know His will for your life may seek to influence you. Their questioning voices and advice can add confusion. Only God knows the plans He has for you. Friends can speculate, but the one Person who knows the truth is also the same Person who loves you and only wants the best for you—the Lord Jesus Christ.

With this in mind, let me ask you: What is holding you back from giving your life completely to Him? Is there anything that this world has to offer that God cannot provide? There is nothing. Love, hope, security, a future, protection, and provision for all your needs—all you could hope to have and experience is wrapped up in Jesus Christ. Will you give Him your life and allow Him to move you forward to a wondrous new place of blessings?

CHAPTER FIVE

Charting a New Direction

How can you know God's will for your life? How do you know He has a plan for you? Does it matter if you turn right or left at the intersection? Will He rescue you if you make a wrong decision and get off course? Each of us has wondered these same questions. Can we know for sure that God has a course laid out for us to follow? Is it important to do His will, or can we simply follow the line of thinking that many have adopted—one that says since we have accepted Christ as Savior, it really does not matter?

There are reasons why people become emotionally, mentally, and physically stuck in reverse. Sometimes this is caused by a lack of obedience because we think we know better than God. We may never admit it, but essentially, when we refuse to submit our lives to Him, we are saying no to His guidance and lordship. We also fall into disobedience when we become complacent about His principles in our lives.

Part of the Plan: A New Beginning

Salvation is a part of the Christian life. It is the starting point, but by no means an ending. Many believers begin the journey into knowing God better, but something happens along the way and they end up abandoning the course. Either they become disappointed, or they are tempted by the sinful pleasures of this world and end up drifting away from God.

When we accept Christ as our Savior, God gives us a new life, a new perspective, and a new sense of hope. He invests in our future. Paul writes, "If anyone is in Christ, he is a new creature; the old things passed away; behold, new things have come" (2 Cor. 5:17). The old way of doing things passes away.

Will there be times when we step back and do some of the very things that once brought heartache to our lives? More than likely we will. However, there is a difference now. We are no longer under the powerful influence of sin unless we choose to be. Sin's power has been broken in our lives. Jesus did this for us on Calvary's cross.

We have done nothing to deserve God's wondrous

grace. It is a gift, and it is the very thing that transforms our lives from being filled with guilt and shame to being reflections of His love, mercy, and forgiveness. He set us free from the bondage of sin so we do not have to live life in reverse. We can live moving forward and not backward.

Some people do not live as if they belong to Jesus because they continue to be influenced by the sinfulness of this world. Each day we have countless encounters that could lead to disobedience. We can say no to sin and no to any activity that is displeasing to the Lord.

Adam and Eve did not make the right decision. God had given them the knowledge they needed to say no to sin. Satan, on the other hand, deceived them into doubting God's goodness. They ended up believing the enemy's lies, and the result of their decision was irrevocable.

God gives each one of us a limited free will. This means we have the limited ability to choose right from wrong. Ultimately He is in control of all things. However, He allows us to make certain decisions. The question becomes, will we chose His way or Satan's?

We can become so persuaded by the enemy's entrapments that we fail to discern the Lord's truth. This is exactly what Adam and Eve did. As a consequence of their wrong decision, the garden of Eden was closed to them, and they were never allowed to walk through its rich, lush pastures again.

This would have been a sorrowful ending to their story except we know the love of God is greater than any sin. He never gave up on them, and He never gives up on us. We may spend years traveling in the wrong direction—living in sin and separated from God. Yet the moment we turn back to Him, He comes to us and washes us in His purity, bathes us with His holiness, and lifts us up so we can begin a new journey—one that moves forward and is abundant in every way (Isa. 1:18).

Dedicating Ourselves to God

Hannah prayed and asked God to give her a son. She was barren and fought feelings of disgrace. God heard her prayer, and she gave birth to a son she named Samuel. He became one of Israel's greatest prophets. She had promised God that if He would allow her to have a son, she would give him to the work of the Lord. After her son's birth, Hannah went to her husband and told him what she had done. He replied, "Do what seems best to you. . . . Only may the LORD confirm His word" (1 Sam. 1:23).

Hannah knew she had her answer, and later, after the boy had grown, she took him to the temple. She told Eli the priest, "Oh, my lord! As your soul lives, my lord, I am the woman who stood here beside you, praying to the LORD. For this boy I prayed, and the LORD has given me my petition which I asked of Him. So I have also dedicated him to the LORD; as long as he lives he is dedicated to the LORD" (1 Sam. 1:26–28).

Hannah gave up something she longed to have in order to receive a richer gain. She gave God her greatest desire—to have a son. In return, He honored her for her sacrifice. Men and women who offer their lives as living sacrifices never travel in reverse. They are forward in their thinking, and they travel spiritual light-years in front of those who are stalled in their devotion to God.

My mother prayed with me every night—not just about my future, but about the things that meant the most to me and to our family. She never told me she wanted me to be a pastor, though one day I overheard her saying that she felt as though this could be the direction God would lead me. Her immediate goals for me were that I would have a desire for my life to count for the Lord and that I would go to school and receive an education.

She only wanted the very best for me. And this is what we should desire for our children and grandchildren. We need to teach them that they can accomplish all things through Christ who provides the opportunity, strength, wisdom, guidance, and hope for every situation they will face today and forever. But far too often the theme song of our world is "Don't Fence Me In." We want to be free to live the way we want to live without any consequences, and this will never happen.

What are you holding on to that God wants? Is it a habit, a relationship, a desire, a dream, a deep passion, or something else? These are the very things that can prevent us from moving in the direction the Lord has chosen for us. In fact, these obstacles can stop us from moving and cause us to feel hopeless.

It is interesting how many people hold on to a relationship or something of material value as if God could not take it away in an instant. One man said to me, "I have worked all my life and saved for what I have. I have two homes and two nice cars, a boat, and the ability to travel around the world. I can't afford to give to God, or I could end up with less than I have."

Actually, we cannot afford to disobey God. Jesus told His disciples a profound story that emphasizes the root of this problem:

> "The land of a rich man was very productive. And he began reasoning to himself, saying, 'What shall I do, since I have no place to store my crops?' Then he said, 'This is what I will do: I will tear down my barns and build larger

ones, and there I will store all my grain and my goods. And I will say to my soul, 'Soul, you have many goods laid up for many years to come; take your ease, eat, drink and be merry.' But God said to him, 'You fool! This very night your soul is required of you; and now who will own what you have prepared?' So is the man who stores up treasure for himself, and is not rich toward God." (Luke 12:16–21)

There is nothing wrong with having money and material possessions. However, when these become the focus of our lives, God usually ends up in second, third, or an even lower place.

The point of the parable is not to condemn someone for having money. God gives us good things. Instead, it was told to point out the attitude of this man's heart. He was not God-focused; he was self-focused, saying, "I will build, and I will enjoy." But there was no mention of God or a desire to honor Him. Jesus admonishes us to give to the Lord, and then He will provide all that we need in return. Giving is an act of worship, submission, and most of all obedience. It reveals our level of faith in God and our desire to yield ourselves to Him.

People who are traveling in reverse rarely think about how they can honor God by giving to Him. Or if they do give, they do so with an attitude of pride, hoping others will see what they have done and be impressed. Giving is an opportunity for us to lift up our hands and open them wide to the Lord, saying, "Lord, all that I have is Yours. You are the One who has given all things, and I offer all that I have and all that I am up to You, asking that You will use it and me in whatever way You choose."

Sadly, Adam and Eve did not make this choice. They became captivated by the idea of knowing as much as God. They envisioned having more than they had been given. The Lord never wanted them to experience the sorrow sin brings, but this is what happened. Nor did He want them to face physical death and the brokenness of their dreams. However, they experienced grievous loss, sorrow, death, and endless frustration as they toiled and labored in a fallen world.

They closed their minds to God's plan for their lives. Once they were moving forward, but then they began a backward spiral until the Lord stepped onto the scene.

Open Up God's Map

During his first missionary trip, Paul traveled through several cities in Galatia, then crossed a portion of the Mediterranean Sea to Antioch. From there he traveled to the island of Cyprus and back to Galatia.

By his second journey, he had learned the art of planning for a long trip. He mapped out his destinations, and when he felt the timing was right, he headed northwest through portions of Galatia and Phrygia. With the better part of the trip in front of him, Paul hit his first snag. As his party tried to travel south into Asia, he found himself being "forbidden" by the Holy Spirit to speak a word in the region.

We can imagine Paul stopping along the roadway, pulling out his maps, double-checking what he had written in order to see if he was following the right route. Feeling affirmed that he was, he pushed forward and tried a second time to enter the region in order to preach the gospel to a group of people he knew needed to hear the truth of God.

What could possibly be wrong with his plans? Didn't God instruct him to take the gospel message first to the Jews and then to the Gentiles? Yes. However, God reserves the right to change our course—at any point and at any time and for any reason.

God's timing is always perfect. Once again Paul tried to enter the region but was blocked by "the Spirit of Jesus," and it became obvious that God had different plans than the ones Paul had written down (Acts 16:6). Therefore the apostle traveled northwest to the city of Troas. During the night he was there, he had a vision of a man "standing and appealing to him, and saying, 'Come over to Macedonia and help us'" (Acts 16:9).

This was all the instruction Paul needed. By early light he ordered the campfires doused with water and everyone's bags packed. They had clear guidance from God, and they were off to do His will. From the city of Troas, they boarded a ship and sailed toward Macedonia. The following day they landed at Neapolis, and from there they went to Philippi, a leading city and a Roman colony in Macedonia.

Have you ever sensed God's Spirit telling you to stop doing what you are doing? No matter how long you continue to press the issue with Him, the answer is still the same—either wait or no. Many people ignore His warning and continue going in the direction opposite of His will. Though hardships may block their way, they continue along a roadway that leads away from God's will. Just because we are moving does not mean we are moving forward. In fact, when we disobey God, our forward progress is stopped.

Paul, however, was committed to obeying the Lord. When he sensed the Lord blocking his efforts, he stopped and waited for guidance. Although he paused, his life never shifted into reverse. This is because Paul's heart was set on doing God's will God's way.

As a result of his actions, the Lord began to move. Paul

took the gospel message west into an area where it had never been preached. Today we have the truth of God's Word mainly because of the faithfulness and obedience of this man and the men and women who came after him. Paul never hesitated, stopped, or demanded his way. Later the Lord allowed His truth to be preached throughout Asia—Paul's original choice for his second missionary journey—and the impact was tremendous.

Had Paul decided he knew better than God, his missionary efforts would have come to a halt. Paul, however, was committed to the Lord. The key to his success was not human talent or reasoning. It was an insatiable desire to obey God and to know Him.

How do we miss God's purpose and plan for our lives?

- We ignore God's call.
- We push to gain our way or reach our own goal.
- We overlook the depth of God's love for us.

I remember sitting on the porch of a man who was about to get married. I knew the situation and wanted to warn him that he could be headed for trouble. I told him, "You need to ask God what you should do."

I started to continue talking, but he stopped me and said, "I hear what you are saying, but I'm going to do it anyway." He deliberately and willfully chose to ignore wise counsel and also God's Word. The marriage lasted exactly six weeks.

I thought, *Well, I know that he has learned a hard lesson.* However, I soon heard that he was going to do the same thing over again. In fact, he continued along this path, making one wrong decision after another.

Some people really do not know the way God wants them to travel. All of us come to a point or a crossroad when we have to stop and ask, "Lord, show me what You want for my life." Paul did the same thing, and the Holy Spirit redirected him in the way he needed to go.

Are you open to what God wants to do in your life? Do you believe that He can use you and also bless you if you will obey Him? Self-will can keep you from experiencing His best. If Paul had resisted, he would have missed a tremendous blessing. After obeying the Lord, not only did he move into a region that needed to hear about the saving grace of God, but also gained a lifelong friend in Luke, who began to travel with him for most of the rest of his life.

You may be thinking, *I can't let go.* You may be determined to do what you want to do. If this is the case, you need to know that God will allow you to go as far as you have to go in order to bring you back home.

CHAPTER SIX

A Long Way from Home

The nights seemed longer than he ever imagined they would be. No—this was not the way he had envisioned life would turn out. He rolled over on his bedroll and tried to find a comfortable position, but it was no use. The ground was hard and unforgiving. The smell of livestock, wet earth, and filth penetrated his nose, mind, and emotions.

Physically, he felt nauseated. Sweat beads trickled down from his temples and mixed with a single line of tears. Emotionally, he was frightened, and for the first time in his life, he did not know what the next day would bring. Would he lose his job—feeding pigs—and end up back on the street having nothing to eat, no place to sleep, and no hope for the future?

He turned over and stared up into the small shelter that

had been built solely to house livestock and not a human being. A hole in the tattered roof allowed him to view a distant star. Suddenly it all came rushing back to him—the thoughts of home and his family. He remembered what it felt like to be living at his father's house. He could almost smell the sweet grass before it was cut in late summer. Closing his eyes, he imagined his hands gently running across the tops of wheat buds ready to be harvested and then winnowed. The freshness of the memory of the old bed beneath him brought a new surge of emotion.

Were his surroundings or the thought of what he had done causing him to feel this way? In a thoughtless moment of rebellion against those he loved, he had asked for his inheritance, packed his bags, and left behind the most precious of gifts, though he did not know it at the time, a father's love. If only he could tell his father that he was sorry, that he was wrong, and that he wanted to come home.

The sudden stir of an animal's hoof broke into his thoughts, and sorrow reclaimed its place in his heart. Though he fought against feelings of despair and depression, he could not help but chide himself over his thoughtless deeds. He had spent his inheritance wildly and without reason—never stopping to think that one day it would be gone. Women befriended him, men envied him, and merchants did not hesitate to entice him with their waves.

However, the moment the money was gone, the celebration over his sinful ways came to a stunning halt. No one bothered to greet him any longer. And no one seemed to care whether he lived or died. Did his father still care?

As he sat up in the darkness, he began to wonder, *Could I go home—work in my father's fields with the hired hands?* His stomach felt uneasy. Dinner the night before had been no more than what he had been able to wrestle away from one of the bulging swine. Pulling his cloak around his shoulders, he stood—stiff and weak—but with a new resolve. He would return home and ask his father to forgive him. He would do anything to go home and be with those he loved.

God Extends His Grace to Us

When you kneel to pray, do you find yourself going back over old sins—failures that happened years ago, or perhaps recent ones that have left you feeling hopeless and alone? You begin to pray but conclude God will not forgive you, and you do not know what to do. You have asked for His forgiveness in the past, but you have ended up feeling as though He does not love you, does not care, and will not forgive your sin. These are Satan's lies. God always forgives, always restores, always loves, and always welcomes us home.

The people whose lives become stuck in reverse often end up in that position because they have chosen to take a route other than the one God wants them to travel. It could be a road to gossip, unforgiveness, a hardened heart, anger, adultery, fornication, or any number of other sins. Anything that separates us from God is sin in His eyes. This is because sin causes us to act independently of the will of God. Anytime we make a decision without consulting the Lord, we risk stepping outside of His will.

Often we think that we need to tackle life the way we want to tackle it. We feel as though we know the true score, and God has not moved a finger to settle the issue that is bothering us. Therefore we take matters into our own hands.

When we begin to view life from this perspective, an alarm should go off inside of us, but like the young man in the story at the beginning of this chapter, it rarely does until it is too late. We often refuse to stop and think about what is waiting for us around the next corner. In the prodigal's case, we can imagine that people lined up to gain access to his inheritance; then a famine hit the region, and his bank account, which was once very large, dwindled to nothing.

Sometimes I run into a person who tells me, "I was once committed to God, but something happened. I changed or He changed or something, but it's just not like it once was between us. I don't feel like He cares for me."

God will never stop loving you. Nothing you can do has the power to derail His love. If there seems to be a distance between you and Him, then it is because you have moved in your devotion, trust, or love for Him. He is the same yesterday, today, and forever (Heb. 13:8).

Satan, however, will do all he possibly can do to remind you of past sin—sin that you have asked God to forgive. He will tell you the Lord is disappointed in you and that there is distance between you and Him. Never believe a word of this. God is intimately involved in the lives of His creation, and He is always close to you. If you have yielded to sin, then you will sense a distance between you and the Lord. But the distance is not because God has moved. He remains the same in His loving care for you. We are the ones who move whenever we choose to disobey the Lord. Sin creates a distance within our hearts. James writes, "Submit therefore to God. Resist the devil and he will flee from you. Draw near to God and He will draw near to you" (4:7–8).

The story of the prodigal son told by Jesus in Luke 15:11–32 is one of the clearest portrayals of God's love, forgiveness, and grace that we have in the Bible. Each one of us at some point has done exactly what the prodigal son did—turned and walked away from God through sin. We may not have physically moved, but emotionally we turned and decided we knew what was best for our lives. We ignored the Lord's principles, plans, or purposes, and we have suffered for our decisions. We have chosen not to obey His commandments and then wondered why our lives have ended up in such disrepair.

Luke records the parable Jesus told His disciples. He begins the story this way:

> "A man had two sons. The younger of them said to his father, 'Father, give me the share of the estate that falls to me.' So he divided his wealth between them. And not many days later, the younger son gathered everything together and went on a journey into a distant country, and there he squandered his estate with loose living. Now when he had spent everything, a severe famine occurred in that country, and he began to be impoverished. So he went and hired himself out to one of the citizens of that country, and he sent him into his fields to feed swine. And he would have gladly filled his stomach with the pods that the swine were eating, and no one was giving anything to him." (15:11–16)

Jesus told this parable so that His followers would have an accurate portrayal of His heavenly Father's love and grace. Many had wondered what God was like. Christ's description in this story was certainly unlike anything they had been taught. Their lives had been steeped in Jewish tradition and following the letter of the law of Moses.

Jesus, however, portrayed God as a loving, forgiving, tenderhearted Father who understands our weaknesses and frailties. He is Someone who hears our prayers and our cries for help. He forgives sin, fills us with His Spirit, and restores us so we can learn to love Him better and honor His name in all that we do.

Many times we fail to sense God's love because our hearts are burdened with false guilt over past mistakes we have made. However, once we pray and ask God to forgive us, He does. He never brings up our sin again. He will not point His finger at us and say, "Remember when you sinned here or failed to keep My commandment there?" This is what the devil does to prevent us from growing in our love and devotion to God. He accuses us and seeks to discourage us so we will want to run away from the Lord.

Condemnation is not from God (Rom. 8:1); it is from the enemy of our souls. The Lord knows we are not perfect. However, He wants us to submit our lives to Him so that He can mold and shape us into the image of His Son.

When we come to Him seeking His forgiveness and restoration, He gives it, not because we deserve it, but because of His love and grace toward us. Grace is His unmerited favor. It is given to imperfect people who want to live their lives for Him.

Just as God extends His grace to us, He also allows us to walk away from Him even though He knows the future and the consequences that will come as a result of our poor decisions. Many times He does not stop us even though He knows we will suffer disappointment. He is committed to disciplining and training us so we will follow Him and not our own plans or desires.

He knows what is best for us and what will bring the greatest sense of joy to our hearts. Therefore, if we insist on doing something that is not part of His will, He will warn us—once, twice, or many more times—before He releases us to our own failure. Throughout the process, He never withdraws His love from us. Yet He knows we are the ones who must choose to obey and trust Him, or we will spend a lifetime steeped in deep sorrow and regret.

A Series of Wrong Steps

Abraham made a choice to follow God. David obeyed the Lord. Joshua trusted Him, and all these and many more men and women found Him faithful. The prodigal son, however, failed to do this. He walked away from his father and everything that was good. Overnight he began to live a life that was stuck in reverse. However, he did not get to a point of utter despair with one step. A series of steps led to his ruin, and these are the same ones we often take.

We have wrong desires. All sin begins in the mind with a desire. There are many times when God gives us good desires—things that bring honor to Him and are blessings to us. There are also times when we face temptation and must choose to obey or disobey the Lord.

The young man in our story did not obey. He had a desire to live the way he wanted to live—independent of his father and his rules. His decision to leave probably had been brewing in his heart for a long time. Sin usually does. Then one day he decided to act on his desire and leave.

God often allows us to be in circumstances that foster tension. We have made a wrong choice—headed off in a wrong direction—and the pressure and stress we feel are the result of His discipline. He does this not to harm us but to teach us how to follow only Him.

Perhaps you are facing a very difficult situation. You have thought about moving on even though you know God has placed you right where you are. You tell yourself that it does not matter what you do next, but it does. Our choices help to shape our lives.

If wrong desires go unchecked, they will lead to some form of action. When something you want to do is not God's best, you need to stop. In fact, never allow any thought to linger in your mind if you know it will end with sin. The cost of disobedience is not worth the price you will pay—broken fellowship with God and others.

If you are not sure that what you are about to do is right, ask God to reaffirm His will for you. There is nothing wrong with going back to Him in prayer. Tell Him that you feel tempted and you need His strength in order to overcome the temptation. This is the way you defeat temptation and sin—by turning to God and asking for His help and strength. He knows your struggle, and if you will come to Him, He will give you the guidance you need to get through any situation.

Remember, the author of Proverbs writes, "In all your ways acknowledge Him, and He will make your paths straight. Do not be wise in your own eyes; fear the LORD and turn away from evil. It will be healing to your body and refreshment to your bones" (3:6–8).

We make wrong decisions. Satan will never tell you about the consequences. He always wants to tell you about what you are feeling and how unfair the circumstances are or how your needs should be met. Only the Spirit of God will warn you about the consequences of sin and disobedience. The prodigal walked away from his father's love and the very things he longed to have—security and a future.

All too often we do the same thing. We abandon God's will for what we think will be greener pastures, but this is never the case. Sin may seem pleasurable for a season, but sooner rather than later, we find out the truth and also the price of our rebellion. The issue at stake is whether we will do whatever we feel is best or whether we will obey the Lord. The decision to walk away from God is always a disastrous one.

We leave the things that God has given us. The prodigal son had only one thing on his mind, and that was to go forward with his misguided plans. He acted on his wrong decisions. There comes a time when God figuratively steps back and allows us to press by Him in an effort to fulfill our desires. Though He never leaves us, He may stop pressing us to follow Him because He knows we have made up our minds to travel in the wrong direction.

When you and I step away from God, we are stepping away from the Person who is our very life. Like many of us when we take the wrong direction, this young man put distance between himself and the one person who loved him unconditionally, his father. When he realized his mistake, he was far from home. He had departed for another land and entered the world of debt and bondage to others.

We do not have to leave physically to depart mentally, spiritually, and emotionally. All we have to do is make a decision to turn in our mind and travel in reverse.

We become deceived. Deception begins the moment we listen to anything that contradicts God's will or command to us. It clouds our spiritual vision and leaves us questioning the goodness of God. For example, the Lord may have placed you in a certain position on your job, but suddenly the idea passes through your mind that you are not really appreciated.

Satan's deceptive words linger, especially since he sees that you have taken note of a coworker being praised by your manager. It is at this point you can choose either to listen to the enemy's voice of temptation or turn to God for His insight and encouragement. If you continue listening to the wrong voice, you run the risk of becoming negative and cynical. Or you may shut down emotionally and stop talking to others as a display of your disapproval.

Convinced that he was doing the right thing, the prodigal left home and headed for the city where he spent all he had on loose living. Satan wants us to leave home—leave God and travel to another country where we will become involved in things that will end up scarring our souls and stripping away our godly innocence.

From time to time, I hear people say, "I don't want to appear too religious—you know—too good." I always want to ask, "Why not? What is wrong with appearing godly—living your life for the One who loves you with a love that will never evaporate, change, or lose its direction? What is wrong with being loved by a God who knows all about you, accepts you fully and unconditionally, and has promised never to leave you?" If that is appearing to be good, I want more of it. In fact, I want to be that godly and much more—I want to become a reflection of His love, faithfulness, and goodness to others. This should be our prayer each and every day.

Deception only leads in one direction—away from God and along a pathway of sorrow and disappointment. It is sent from the enemy with a purpose: to cause confusion and prevent us from being all that the Lord wants us to become. He has a plan for each one of us. It is one of hope and purpose. Satan, however, knows this and responds accordingly by setting traps of deception to derail us with sin. He wants us to fail, knowing that when we do, he will begin to condemn and belittle us.

We experience defeat and heartache. Sin leaves us spiritually, emotionally, morally, and physically bankrupt. No sooner had this young man spent all he had on worldly, empty pleasures than famine swept over the land. Suddenly he had nothing. His money was gone. His relationship with his family was broken. Any friendships he had established when he was living without restraint had dissolved, and he found himself seeking employment in the lowest possible position—feeding pigs!

Sin destroys, but God restores. There will be times when we have to experience the consequences of our sin to realize the mistakes we have made. If we sin and life continues on without a problem, we will continue the wrong behavior. God has to allow us to feel the weight of our sin so that we will acknowledge it before him and turn away from it.

We sink into feelings of despair. Life became so miserable for the prodigal that he did the unthinkable. He was Jewish, and yet, he went to work for a Gentile hog herder. This was the lowest occupation a Jewish boy could have had. It also is a picture of utter desperation. In fact, the Bible seems to indicate that he wrestled to get the pods that had fallen off the trees away from the pigs because he had nothing else to eat. No one would help him, and he was operating in total despair. This is the natural progression of sin. It all begins with a wrong thought or desire. Then we are tempted to make a bad decision, which means we have been deceived. This is when we suffer defeat and despair.

The final step is one of desperation. Anything that drives you back to God is good for you. If desperation is a necessary step in order for you to come to your senses, then it is a good step.

Jesus said, "When [this young man] came to his senses, he said, 'How many of my father's hired men have more than enough bread, but I am dying here with hunger! I will get up and go to my father, and will say to him, "Father, I have sinned against heaven, and in your sight; I am no longer worthy to be called your son, make me as one of your hired men."' So he got up and came to his father" (Luke 15:17–20).

One of the worst feelings comes as a result of realizing you have disobeyed the Lord and lost what you really wanted most in life. It also is one of the best because our realization of sin is God's opportunity to turn our lives around—pull us out of reverse and back into His loving care. The prodigal was despairing over what he had done. At that point, it seems as though he did not have any hope—that was until he remembered his father's love. Suddenly a light of hope fell down around him, and he imagined going home and admitting his thoughtless sin. It was at this moment that he repented and desired to be forgiven.

The Greek word for *sin* means to miss the mark. Repentance means that we recognize that what we have done is wrong and we make a conscious decision to turn away from it. In other words, we realize that we are traveling in reverse and do something about it in order to start moving forward again.

This is exactly what the prodigal did. He returned home, and even before he crested the hill near the family home, his father saw him and ran out to meet him. Though we sin and fall short or miss the target, God watches for us to come back to Him, and when we do, He runs to meet us.

The prodigal's father was a man of great wealth, and rarely if ever did he have an occasion to run to greet anyone. He was a man of position, and people bowed in honor to him. However, when he saw his son coming back to him, not the "son" who left home in rebellion, but one who had been humbled by the consequences of his sin, he ran to meet him.

How do we know the boy meant business? He got up and left. A lot of people get in situations that are beyond their ability to control. They have fallen into sin, and rather than cry out to God for help, they keep looking for a way around the problem. They keep thinking things will get better, but they only get worse.

If you have yielded to sin and now find yourself far from home—desperate and disillusioned—you can turn back right now. You do not have to continue driving in the wrong direction. You can stop and tell the Lord that what you have done is wrong and you recognize it. You do not have to have a plan to reverse your steps. In fact, it is better just to lay your life down and tell Him that you were wrong and need His help. Ask Him to take over the affairs of your life and lead you home again.

When you cry out to Him, He always answers.

CHAPTER SEVEN

Restored by Grace

Immediately before Jesus told the parable of the prodigal son, He told the story of the lost sheep. He was setting the stage for the story of God's eternal love and restoration. The Lord rejoices at the sound of our repentance because He knows that when we turn back to Him, we are developing a heart for His principles and truth.

Christ said,

"What man among you, if he has a hundred sheep and has lost one of them, does not leave the ninety-nine in the open pasture and go after the one which is lost until he finds it? When he has found it, he lays it on his shoulders, rejoicing. And when he comes home, he calls together his friends and his neighbors, saying to them, 'Rejoice with me, for I have found my sheep which was lost!' I tell you that in the same way, there will be more joy in heaven over one sinner who repents than over ninety-nine righteous persons who need no repentance." (Luke 15:4–7)

The person who sincerely comes to God is never turned away. He even hears the prayers of those who are trying to bargain with Him. Some of us may pray, "Lord, if You will just get me out of this mess, I will never disobey You again." But we do. However, God may straighten out our circumstances, not as a result of our selfish prayers, but because He longs to give us another opportunity to abandon our self-driven desires in order to live fully for Him. You have no idea what God can do with your life if you will give yourself to Him. The potential is endless because He is infinite in power and only desires our very best. Unfortunately, many people have not grasped this fact. They reason that they must get ahead in life, and if they spend time with God, they will be held back because God's ways are too good, too simple, or uncreative. And yet no one has more creative power than the Lord. He created the universe and all that is in it. He will certainly be creative in your life.

When we are unwilling to submit ourselves to the authority of God, sin binds us. The chains of adultery entrap us and prevent us from living free and enjoying life the way God intends for us to enjoy it. Drugs and alcohol blind us to God's providential care. Money and the desire to have more bring stress and havoc along with the need for power, control, and status. Instead of being under God's rule, we are being ruled by the very things that keep us bound in darkness. We could list many things that we allow to occupy the place that only God should hold within our hearts. Thankfully, God freely offers us His grace, which covers all of our sins and releases us from their bondage.

God's Grace Is Sufficient

The prodigal came face-to-face with these same temptations. His soul was steeped in thoughts of selfishness. However, when he lost everything, he came to his senses and said, "I will return to my father. I will go back. I will humble myself and do whatever it takes to make things right between me and him because I realize I love him."

Genuine repentance says, "I'm going to turn around and head in the opposite direction. I'm making a decision to go home and start over." He had wasted years of his life along with his talents and gifts. Everything was squandered on an immoral lifestyle, and he had absolutely nothing left, but he turned around and headed back home.

And his father was waiting for him with his arms open wide. The son arrived with nothing. In fact, he probably did not even have a decent pair of sandals because, along with a robe, his father gave him a pair (Luke 15:22). The father clothed his repentant son, just as God clothed Adam and Eve after they had sinned and been cast out of the garden of Eden. The love of God covers us in our sorrow as we acknowledge our sin to Him (Prov. 10:12).

Do you believe you can sin so badly and sink so low that you are beyond any hope? I want to assure you that nothing you will ever do will change God's love for you. He loves you unconditionally, and His grace is sufficient for every trial and disappointment you face (2 Cor. 12:9). It is also sufficient for the times you know you have taken the wrong road and headed off in sin's direction. Whatever comes your way, God will give you the power and wisdom you need to handle it. He will provide the reassurance you need to live in light of His forgiveness. He is able and more than willing to guide and protect you as you go through each day. When you do yield to sin, He allows the consequences of your decisions to work in a way that will bring you back to Him. This is not the result of His anger toward you but is evidence of His grace reaching out to bring you home.

Some people spend their entire lifetime running away

from God and living in horrendous situations. Feelings of guilt can prevent us from coming home, but grace welcomes us with open arms. Just like the father in this story, God is waiting for us to turn back to Him whenever we take a wrong turn or pathway. He looks for our return, and when He sees us, He rushes to embrace us. But there are countless individuals who never return home because they do not believe God loves them and has forgiven them.

God's love for us does not involve what we do or do not do. He loves us because this is His nature. "God is love, and the one who abides in love abides in God, and God abides in him. . . . There is no fear in love; but perfect love casts out fear, because fear involves punishment, and the one who fears is not perfected in love. We love, because He first loved us" (1 John 4:16, 18–19). Performance may work for the world, but it only creates frustration for the child of God. This is because God's gift of love and grace is given, not because of what we have done, but because of the One we know and love intimately—the Lord Jesus Christ. There is nothing we can do to earn more of God's love. We have all of it. In fact, the moment we ask Him to come into our lives, we receive all God has to give us.

However, many people continue throughout their lives believing if they can "do" something good enough for

God, then He will accept them. There is nothing that can make us more acceptable to Him. He accepts us just the way we are—with all our flaws and failures. The one thing that draws us to God is our desire to know and experience His personal and intimate love.

Moses Turned and God Responded

Think about Moses. The moment he turned to look at the burning bush, God spoke to him (Exod. 3:3–4). The Lord knew he was ready to serve Him and not his own personal desires. Moses developed a heart for God in the wilderness, and we can too. Obeying God consumed Moses' life, and he became the man God chose to lead His people out of Egyptian captivity and to the doorstep of the Promised Land.

Sometimes, even when our lives appear to be stuck in reverse, God is preparing us for something greater. In fact, He is always at work in our lives. We may run into difficulty that seems so dark and foreboding it causes us to wonder if we will be able to continue. Feelings of despair seek to rob us of all hope, but just when we feel as though the darkness will consume us, God's light of love breaks through—rescuing us and making a way for us to travel through the wilderness of our shattered dreams and into His arms of forgiveness.

The only way a person remains frozen in reverse is if he or she chooses to stay in this position. God's grace—His unmerited favor—is the key that unlocks the prison door, which has separated us from His goodness and love. His grace cannot be manipulated nor can it be purchased. It is an eternal expression of His wondrous, divine favor toward us.

A primary reason people have difficulty believing this is because they have never experienced the unconditional love of God. They cannot imagine Him loving them because of what their past contains, but He does. They think, *Surely I have to do something to earn the love and forgiveness of God. Just asking and meaning it seems too simple.* Salvation is really very simple. It is a matter of acknowledging your need for a Savior—God's Son (John 3:26). It also involves admitting that you have sinned against Him—just like the prodigal did. However, we must also accept His love. Think about how differently this story would have turned out if the prodigal had decided not to go home because the shame was too great or he could not accept his father's love because he felt so unworthy.

We must learn to accept the gift of God's grace, and this is where many people get tripped up. They do not know how to accept His love. Chances are they do not know how to accept the love of others either. Pride tells us, "Oh no. You can't love me because I have done something far too horrible." It also tempts us to feel obligated when someone is nice to us. There are people who cannot accept a gift without thinking, *I'll give you something in return.* When we truly learn to love, we also know how to give and receive the way God intended.

Pride is the thing that captured Satan's heart and caused him to lose his position before God. He was the most beautiful of all the angels—created by God for His glory and to worship Him (Isa. 14:12). However, he invited pride into his heart thinking that he would become more powerful, more wonderful, and greater than God. Actually, he wanted to rule over God, and this led to his rapid downfall. He fell from his place of great service to earth where he continues his wicked schemes against God's creation today. Yet his end is sure. He is doomed to be overthrown by the Lord and His hosts (Rev. 19:20).

The Signet Ring

The wonderful thing about our heavenly Father's love is that it is unconditional. As Jesus told the parables of the lost sheep and the prodigal son, He made it clear that our heavenly Father welcomes us home because He never stops loving us. The son's return restored the fellowship that was broken. Why do people fail to recognize that things are not right and they are living life stuck in reverse?

First, they have never experienced the unconditional love of God. For whatever reason, they have either ignored God's call or put off responding to it. Therefore, they have fallen into sin and failed to realize there is hope for their lives. Instead of stepping free of the bondage, they remain captured by it. Many people do not even realize they are trapped until it seems too late. But it is never too late when God is involved. Nothing is impossible with Him (Luke 1:37). He can free us from the deepest sin, as well as from feelings of hopelessness and despair.

For people who have spent years feeling depressed, God wants you to know you are loved and can be free of your sense of shame and false guilt. Both of these can hold you back from being all God wants you to be. They can keep you in a perpetual reverse state. God, however, does not want you living in this type of darkness. He will not withhold His love from you. When you tell Him that you love Him, He responds with abundant love.

Second, people do not believe God will accept them. They may feel embarrassed about their sin and stuff it deep down inside of themselves. They hope for the best rather than pray, "Lord, I have messed up my life. I have tried to live for myself and only ended up feeling lonely, lost, and afraid. I want to get things right with You. How do I do this?"

You do not have to beg God to forgive your sin. You do not have to make promises about what you are going to do. God is listening for a simple, genuine confession saying that you have sinned and you need His help. He wants to restore you. In fact, that is His desire for each one of us—to restore us to our rightful relationship with Him.

What was the father's attitude in the story of the prodigal son? Did he belittle his son? No. Did he go over a long list of things that the son had done and how these had resulted in hardship for the family? Absolutely not! Did he try to produce guilt within his son by telling him how he had caused heartache in his own life? No. He ran out to meet him saying to those who worked for him, "Quickly bring out the best robe and put it on him, and put a ring on his hand and sandals on his feet; and bring the fattened calf, kill it, and let us eat and celebrate; for this son of mine was dead and has come to life again; he was lost and has been found" (Luke 15:22–24).

God's perspective is this: once a son or a daughter, always a son or a daughter—once a saint, always a saint. We may become dirty as a result of costly, wrong decisions and sin, but God will never reject us and never turn us away. This is the way His unconditional fatherly love operates. It always forgives, restores, hopes, and plans for your very best. Besides all of that: His love covers your sinfulness and brings you back into a right relationship with Him (Prov. 10:12).

Someone reading this may be thinking there is something about all of this that seems troubling. After all, isn't it only right for this young man to suffer for what he has done? It appears he has gotten away with sin.

The prodigal did not get away with anything. He lost his inheritance, self-worth, self-esteem, and all that he held dear. Sin stole his joy, sense of peace, and hope for the future. Before he came to his senses, he was working in a position lower than his father's servants.

How can a holy God forgive sin when He knows we have disobeyed Him, become entangled in the worst kind of sin, and refused to come home? There is only one answer to this question, and it is the Cross. This is the reason God forgives each one of us.

Our sin was punished on Calvary's cross when the Lord Jesus Christ died for our sins. He took our place on the cross. It is only by God's mercy and grace that we are forgiven. Conviction, repentance, and salvation are the results of His grace at work in our lives. However, none of these on their own actually bring about change within our lives. The change comes when we recognize our need for a Savior and that our actions, decisions, and motives are wrong and we want to turn away from them.

Understanding this principle will make an eternal difference in the way you live. Once you understand the precious, matchless gift God has given you through His loving grace, you will want to live every day for Him. The single goal of the apostle Paul's life was to live for Jesus Christ. He writes, "Whatever things were gain to me, those things I have counted as loss for the sake of Christ. More than that, I count all things to be loss in view of the surpassing value of knowing Christ Jesus my Lord, for whom I have suffered the loss of all things, and count them but rubbish so that I may gain Christ, and may be found in Him" (Phil. 3:7–9).

The prodigal got up and left for home knowing that he had sinned against his father, and he was tremendously moved with sorrow and regret. He wanted another chance at life. He may have lost his initial inheritance, but he was still a son and he could go home. If you have traveled to a faraway land in order to get away from God, you need to realize several things.

You can never outrun God. No matter how far you run, God knows exactly where you are and His love for you remains constant. David writes,

> Behold, O LORD, You know it all. You have enclosed me behind and before, and laid Your hand upon me. Such knowledge is too wonderful for me. . . .

Where can I go from Your Spirit? Or where can I flee from Your presence? If I ascend to heaven, You are there; if I make my bed in Sheol, behold, You are there. If I take the wings of the dawn, if I dwell in the remotest part of the sea, even there Your hand will lead me, and Your right hand will lay hold of me. (Ps. 139:4–10)

You can never "out sin" the grace of God. He will never look at you and think, *Your sin is too great. I can't keep loving you.* God's desire is that you will not yield to temptation. He knows what sin will do to your life, especially your heart—a heart that was created by Him and for His love. Nothing is greater than God's love for you.

Nothing is more powerful than His grace and ability to love. You cannot stop the love of God—no matter what you do. Are you ready to move forward and experience His unconditional love in a way that you never thought would be possible? If so, take your first step of faith and open your heart to Him.

My prayer is that you will realize His love is a gift that He gives freely to you. Once you have experienced it, you will have the opportunity to live in His eternal freedom and hope. However, if you find yourself entangled in sin, then remember: God still loves you. The circumstances of this world cannot change this fact. They may prevent you from enjoying the love that has been given to you, but nothing is strong enough to dilute the love of God. If you have never accepted Him as your Savior, then you can do this right now.

God wants you to come home to Him. The story of the prodigal son contains a powerful truth. God is watching, waiting, and longing for us to turn back to Him. Perhaps you have not gone away. Then His desire is for you to draw even closer to His flame of love.

If you have been away for a long time, and after reading this decide it is time to go home—back to His love and to the familiar embrace of His matchless peace—then I want to ask you, what is holding you back? Right now, wherever you are sitting or standing, you can turn and start walking home.

I cannot imagine what this young man felt like when he crested the hill on the road to his family's home. Suddenly, in the distance he saw his father running out to meet him with arms wide open. This is exactly what God will do when He sees you running to Him.

CHAPTER EIGHT

Facing Detours and Roadblocks

The trials and pressures of life can become roadblocks to God's plan for our lives. Israel came to a huge roadblock when they approached the Red Sea. They only had a couple of choices: either they could stay where they were—on the shoreline and be killed or recaptured by the Egyptian army—or they could move forward into the water and trust God to open up the way before them.

There are many times in life when we feel closed in on all sides. We do not know which way to turn. When this happens there is only one thing to do, and that is to pray. Really, prayer is not an option. It needs to be our first response in times of trouble as well as in moments of joy. This was especially true in Israel's case since their enemies were bearing down on them. Moses and the people cried out to God, but their cries were ones of panic and not of faith in an all-knowing, all-powerful God. "Then the LORD said to Moses, 'Why are you crying out to Me? Tell the sons of Israel to go forward. As for you, lift up your staff and stretch out your hand over the sea and divide it, and the sons of Israel shall go through the midst of the sea on dry land'" (Exod. 14:15–16).

Feelings of fear and hopelessness can paralyze us and prevent us from going forward and doing what God has called us to do. God gave Moses insight into His plan. He told him that He was going to harden Pharaoh's heart to an even greater degree so that he would be compelled to follow God's people in order to destroy them.

However, this pursuing enemy would never get close enough to harm them. Why did God allow the enemy to follow Israel? For one reason: He wanted them to see His power displayed and understand that there is no God like Him. He wanted Israel to depend only on Him. This is His goal for each one of our lives.

There is nothing in His Word that tells us living for Him will be easy and free of trouble. In fact, the opposite may well be true. Often God allows us to face trials to strengthen our faith and remind us of His personal work in our lives. If life were free of trouble and heartache, we would be tempted to think that we do not need Him. But we do—not just occasionally, but every moment of every day. We need to know He is near and that He is guiding us.

The nation of Israel had not learned this. This is why God set a cloud before them to lead them through the day and a pillar of fire behind them at night. He wanted His people to know He was with them, and He gave them physical evidence of this. Today He has given us the Holy Spirit, who resides inside the life of every believer. He is our infinite guide, comforter, and the one Person who leads us forward in godly truth (John 16:13).

The Degrees of Faith

The Red Sea did not automatically open up before the people. It was not until Moses approached the water and lifted his hands, holding the staff God had given him, that the waters parted. There will be times in your life when God will require you to step forward by faith not knowing how He will provide the miracle or the answer to your prayers. Regardless of your circumstances, your only concern is to trust Him.

Little faith says, "I think He can do this."

Great faith says, "I know He can."

Perfect faith says, "It is done." In other words, there is no question in your mind of God's ability or faithfulness.

Most people live with an attitude that says, "I think

God can help me." If questioned, they may say, "Oh, I know He can." However, they usually add, "But will He?" This is the point when we get into trouble. Questioning God's ability and love can lead us to doubt His goodness, and then we become confused and even misled.

Many people get stuck in reverse because they do not know which way to go. God has told them to move forward, but they wonder if they can trust Him. They approach a critical junction with feelings of doubt and low self-esteem. Instead of stepping forward and believing God for His best, they hesitate, withdraw, feel bad about themselves, and wither in defeat.

We can never give the enemy an inch. If Israel had not gone forward, they would have disobeyed God and fallen into the hands of their enemies. There was only one way for them to travel, and it was the way of faith, which led straight across the bottom of the Red Sea to the opposite shoreline.

There can be no "what ifs." Like Israel, we should focus our eyes on two things: God's ability within us and His all-powerful provision for us. He was the One who held back the waters of the Red Sea and also the One who provided the strength the people needed to get to the opposite side.

Whatever you are facing, God is beside you, making a way for you to travel through what seems to be impossible circumstances. The question is, do you have little faith, great faith, or perfect faith?

Pharaoh's army followed the people into the Red Sea. However, as soon as the last person of Israel stepped up on dry land on the opposite shore, God closed the waters in and around the enemy. He delivered His people just as He promised.

After Christ's death, the disciples became so discouraged they did not want to continue the mission the Lord had given them. They were stuck emotionally and mentally. Although they had heard the Lord say on several occasions He was going away but would return to them, they did not understand His words (John 12:35-37). In the aftermath of the crucifixion, they became frightened and hid in fear of losing their lives.

Although Jesus spoke of His death and resurrection, His followers were more interested in thinking about the future from their perspective. God, however, had a different set of plans. He knew the steps Christ would take to fulfill His will.

The temptation the disciples battled, as well as the one that Israel faced, was centered on human expectations. God does not always work the way we think He will. In fact, He often chooses a completely different route from the one we would take. As the days passed, the disciples even returned to their previous occupations—the same ones they had before meeting the Savior. Jesus appeared to them early one morning on the shore of the Sea of Galilee where Peter, James, and John were fishing. From their perspective, the vision that had seemed so real a few weeks earlier had vanished—that is until Jesus appeared to them.

They had been fishing for hours and had caught nothing, but suddenly the water began to stir, and their nets began to fill with fish to the point of breaking. In a matter of moments, they went from feeling defeated and abandoned to savoring the mighty victory of Christ's death and resurrection (John 21:1–12).

We can become so stuck in feelings of sorrow and disappointment that we do not want to move forward. God is aware of this. He knows heartache can touch our lives with such power that we want to quit. He also knows and understands the danger that comes from allowing sorrowful feelings to linger for a long time. This is when, if we are not careful, we can become depressed and worried over issues that God has settled for us. After all, He is sovereign, and He will not allow anything to touch our lives that will not ultimately glorify Him and bring a sense of peace and joy to our hearts.

Dealing with Detours

Perhaps the news you received as you left work on Friday was not good. It marked the end of your current employment. However, what came as a surprise or shock to you was not a shock to God. The crucifixion did not take Jesus by surprise. He knew it was coming, and He allowed it to touch His life for a greater purpose, and the same is true for each one of us. Trials come, but not with the intent of destroying us. Instead, God allows them so that He can strengthen us for an even greater challenge.

If you are suffering through the aftermath of the death of a loved one or battling the pain that comes from going through a divorce, then this may not seem to be something you can accept. You may wonder how you will go on another day. God has the answer, and He promises to walk through this valley with you (Ps. 23:4). While the recovery may take some time, you will discover God is with you every step of the way. He gives strength to the weary so they can run and not grow tired (Isa. 40:31).

God has a will for our lives, but we must make the decision to follow Him to discover it and move forward. One young man looked across the room at me and said, "I have waited my entire life to be free from my parents' control. Now that I am old enough, I'm not waiting for God to tell me what to do next. If He wants me to know something, He will tell me."

Anytime we have an "I will" attitude that is not God-centered, we can mark it down that we are headed for trouble. This is because God wants to be the central focus of our lives and our worship.

Most of us can think of a time when we said, "I'm going to do this simply because I feel I have waited long enough, and I deserve it." The truth is, we do not deserve anything. All that we have has been given to us as a gift from God. Everything in heaven and on earth belongs to Him. However, many people today live with a "me first" attitude. They believe society owes them something. Instead of experiencing fulfillment and peace, they live a restless existence, always looking to receive something from someone.

King Saul lived a restless life because he was not fully committed to God. The motivation of his heart was to acquire notoriety and fame, and he was willing to go to any extreme to achieve these.

God anointed him the first king over Israel. However, sin and pride became factors in his disobedience and were obvious detours that took him away from God's plan. We can become sidetracked in the same way. Self-pity, anger, and depression are also detours that block us from doing God's will. They stop our forward progress and shift us back into reverse. At some point, each one of us has to deal with pride. God, however, has a victory waiting for us if we will keep the focus of our lives set on Him and not on our own desires.

We will also face times when we are tempted to think we know better than the Lord. This is exactly what Saul did as a new, young king. In 1 Samuel 15, Saul was instructed to defeat the Amalekites and to destroy all that was theirs, but he did not obey God's command, and the Lord regretted making him king.

God knows the future. He gives us commandments based not on what we perceive to be right but on what He knows is best for us. God knew that if Israel did not completely destroy their enemies, at a later date they would face defeat at the hands of these same people. However, once Saul won the battle, he spared the life of the Amalekite king, who was a dire enemy of the Lord and the nation of Israel. This one decision caused the nation of Israel extreme trouble.

At this point Saul was more interested in appearances than he was in obeying and honoring God. He longed for the people to praise *him* for the victory and not the Lord God. He also spared the best of the flock and the oxen and headed to Carmel where he erected a monument in his honor rather than building one to glorify God. He even performed a sacrifice to God instead of waiting for Samuel's arrival. Saul was in the process of setting himself up to be the sole sovereign over the nation of Israel. Not only would he be king over the people; he would be worshiped as well.

When confronted by the prophet Samuel, Saul did not immediately admit his guilt. Instead, he tried to appear humble and claimed he was doing only what God had commanded him to do. However, Saul was directly contradicting God's command to place no other gods before Him (Exod. 20:3).

There are people who rush off to do God's will, but their hearts do not belong totally to the Lord. They are focused on what they can do—the honor they want to receive along with the title, the corner office, and the larger salary.

God rejected Saul because of self-pride and disobedience. From this moment until the day he died, Saul's life was lived in reverse. What once was a promising beginning ended in sorrow and defeat. Like Saul, we can become determined to live a lifestyle devoted to ourselves and not to God. However, God's grace is given to each one of us when we turn back and seek His forgiveness and restoration. Detours can be avoided because sin is avoidable. You can say no to the very things that are not God's best for you. How do you do this?

Check your heart to make sure your first desire is to follow Christ and not your own desires. Far too many people fail to take adequate time to pray and to seek God. They assume that Either he will approve of all they are doing, or He will give them a "hall pass" from class and not require them to follow His rules and be in attendance.

God has a plan, but it is our responsibility to seek Him and find out what that plan includes. He may show us a large portion of what He wants us to do. Or He may only give us a glimpse into His purpose. It does not really matter how much God reveals to us. When we are driving along His roadway, we will have a sense of peace residing within our hearts. Our lives will not be stuck in reverse. We will move forward and have a sense of joy for the journey.

A lack of peace usually indicates there is a problem. Either we have been unwilling to submit our lives to Him, or the enemy is seeking to reroute us away from God's best. If it is the latter, we need to stand firm in our faith and trust God for His protection and help. Peter reminds us that the devil "prowls around like a roaring lion, seeking someone to devour" (1 Pet. 5:8).

At times, the Lord allows our faith to be tested to strengthen and prepare us for the next step in life. Job was severely tested, Joseph spent years in prison for something he did not do, and David was resigned to running away from a man who was bent on killing him. When difficulty comes, we can look at it one of two ways—either as a roadway to blessing and a closer relationship with God or as something we need to avoid. Always choose to see every problem as an opportunity to know God better and to experience His intimacy in a greater way.

When you run up on a roadblock or detour, ask God to show you what He wants you to learn. There is no way to avoid heartache and sorrow. They are an inescapable part of life. However, they do not have to become points of defeat. Instead, they can become avenues of blessing, hope, and victory, especially when we are willing to learn what God wants to teach us. The prophet Isaiah writes, "[God] gives strength to the weary, and to him who lacks might He increases power. Though youths grow weary and tired, and vigorous young men stumble badly, yet those who wait for the LORD will gain new strength; they will mount up with wings like eagles, they will run and not get tired, they will walk and not become weary" (40:29–31).

There is no reason for us to get stuck in reverse when we have an all-knowing, all-powerful God who loves us with an everlasting love. Job reminds us, "With Him are wisdom and might" (12:13).

Set the focus of your heart on the Lord. Paul writes, "Do not be conformed to this world, but be transformed by the renewing of your mind, so that you may prove what the will of God is, that which is good and acceptable and perfect" (Rom. 12:2). Most athletes know that winning a race or a game does not solely involve sheer physical strength. It involves the right type of training and the correct focus—a fixed focus on the goal or the victory.

How do we renew our minds? We keep our hearts focused on God through prayer and reading the Bible. His Word is the light of wisdom and hope to our pathway. It guides us so we can discover God's purpose, plan, and desires for our lives. A person who is living life in reverse is someone who has not applied God's principles fully to his or her life. When God's Word is hidden within your heart, temptation may come, but God's truth will meet and defeat it. For example, when the enemy tells you that you cannot take advantage of a certain opportunity, the Holy Spirit will contradict the lie by telling you that you can do all things through Him who gives you the strength and wisdom you need for the task (Phil. 4:13).

Anytime we lose sight of God's will and plan for our lives, we risk becoming discouraged and defeated. Gideon had an army that numbered in the thousands, but God had a lesson that He wanted him and the nation of Israel to learn. It was a lesson of faith. Therefore He reduced Gideon's troops from twenty-two thousand to a mere three hundred fighting men. The enemy had a force of thousands, but they did not have the Lord God fighting for them—Israel did and you do too (Judg. 7).

The Lord said to Gideon, "The people who are with you are too many for Me to give Midian into their hands, for Israel would become boastful, saying, 'My own power has delivered me'" (Judg. 7:2). Only God is due all our praise and glory. As we submit our lives to Him, He will position us to do great things for Him, but if we forget who the source of our strength is, we will miss a tremendous blessing and suffer a sincere defeat.

Ask God to help you make wise decisions. The key to living a life of abundant joy and peace is knowing God. Everything is encompassed in this. When given a choice to ask for anything, Solomon asked God for wisdom.

> "In Gibeon the LORD appeared to Solomon in a dream at night; and God said, 'Ask what you wish Me to give you.' Then Solomon said, 'You have shown great lovingkindness to Your servant David my father, according as he walked before You in truth and righteousness and uprightness of heart. . . . So give Your servant an understanding heart to judge Your people to discern between good and evil.'" (1 Kings 3:5–6, 9)

He did not ask for riches or fame or even good health. Solomon prayed and asked for discernment and an understanding heart.

As a result of his desire to know God better and to understand His ways, the Lord told him,

"Because you have asked this thing and have not asked for yourself long life, nor have asked riches for yourself, nor have you asked for the life of your enemies, but have asked for yourself discernment to understand justice, behold, I have done according to your words. Behold, I have given you a wise and discerning heart, so that there has been no one like you before you, nor shall one like you arise after you. I have also given you what you have not asked, both riches and honor, so that there will not be any among the kings like you all your days." (1 Kings 3:11–13)

Do not waste your life thinking about what could have been or how you have been short-changed. In God's economy, wealth and riches are found in knowing and loving Him. When your life is dedicated totally to Him, He will give you the wisdom you need to make right decisions every time. His very character is wisdom.

Realize God's Way Is the Right Way

.ing out to God to show you what you need to do, then you need to be careful and ask Him to make His will very clear to you. You cannot make a decision based solely on the opinion of others or, at times, even the facts that have been given to you. You must be still in your mind and heart before the Lord. There are times when you can listen to a friend's advice, especially if it is godly advice and lines up with the Word of God. However, many times God wants you to seek Him alone and apart from what others may say. He is the One who knows the plans He has for you (Jer. 29:11).

I remember the first time this became very clear to me. I was fifteen and was with several of my friends. We never got into any trouble, yet we were young and adventuresome like most teenagers. We had decided to meet at a local drugstore, which was about a mile away from where I lived. When we got there, we ordered chocolate shakes, and in the course of conversation one of my friends spoke up and suggested that we go to the pool hall just to shoot pool. In those days, pool halls were beer joints. Immediately I felt uneasy and said, "I don't know about that."

Eager to go, my friends began to prod me. One said, "Oh, come on, Stanley. We know you don't drink. We're not going to drink. We're just going to shoot pool."

No matter what they said to me, I continued to feel restless, but they continued to persist. "Nobody's going to see you; don't worry about it. We're just going to have a good time and shoot a little pool."

It was at this point that I sensed God speaking to my heart, saying, "Don't do it."

While it was difficult, I said, "I'm not going with you." They chimed, "Aw, come on. What do you mean, you're not going?" But I held firm to my decision and said, "I'm not going." Then I remember walking away.

The route home took me through a familiar neighborhood that was on my paper route. As I was thinking about what had just happened, I remember stopping outside the home of a man named R. B. Rogers. It was seven fifteen in the evening, and I was on North Main Street. This is where and when I sensed the Lord confirming His words to me and saying, "You will never regret this decision." And I never have.

I am not sure why God did not want me to go that evening. He had a reason, and my only option was to obey Him. I can look back over my life and think of times when I was standing at a crossroad. God would say, "Don't do that," or "Take this road. No matter what you face, keep your eyes focused on Me."

I now understand God was deliberately and willfully

leading me a certain way. He has the advantage of knowing all things and loving us with an unconditional love. Therefore His purpose for our lives always leads to incredible blessing. The same is true for your life each day.

CHAPTER NINE

A Step of Faith

Years ago, whenever I would make a point about God moving us forward, I would often tell my congregation, "God cannot move a parked car!" Most would laugh. However, the look on the faces of many reflected a deep sorrow, probably because they felt as though they were stranded on the side of the road without any hope. No matter how difficult life becomes, God's grace and mercy are greater than any problem we face. There is always hope because there is God. To understand this fully, we must learn to trust Him with the circumstances of our lives.

Peter was able to walk on the water to Jesus until he took his eyes off of the Lord and began to notice the size and strength of the waves surrounding him. Then he began to sink, and as he did, he cried out, "Lord, save me!"

(Matt. 14:30). Jesus reached out and pulled him up out of the water. And then the Lord asked Peter, "You of little faith, why did you doubt?" (v. 31). Why do we doubt God's ability to protect us and provide for every need we have?

Trust Involves a Relationship

Trusting God always involves knowing Him. If you do not have a personal relationship with the Savior, then you will have difficulty trusting Him on any level. Peter knew Jesus. Therefore it was natural for him to want to go to the Savior. He was his Lord, his Friend, and his Teacher. He knew he could trust Him no matter what the circumstances were. Yet he hesitated and looked at what was going on around him. This is when his heart grew fearful. There will be times when we cannot allow our eyes to drift even an inch to the right or the left. If we do, we will begin to sink.

Peter probably realized that he would be walking on a surface that, from a human standpoint, could not support his weight. However, this was not what frightened him. It was the sight of the waves and the pressure of the wind blowing against him that caused him to doubt Christ's ability to keep him safe. We do the same thing when we run to one friend and then another talking about the circumstances of our lives. We use words like "what if" and "but I don't know."

In the beginning, Peter's words were words of faith. Yet when he began to walk to Jesus, he started thinking about what he was facing and doing from a human perspective. The waves were high, the wind was strong, and the night was very dark.

The walk of faith is a walk that is steady and firmly focused on God. There will be times when the Lord only tells us what we need to do or know at the moment. He does not give us the big picture. However, if our steps are ones set on a foundation of faith in Him, we will not sink. In fact, we will achieve the goal and the victory that God has given us.

We may accept a new position on our jobs or enter a relationship that we have longed to have. Our minds are made up; we know God has led us this far. However, as we begin our journey, a problem arises. The atmosphere turns dark and stormy, and we feel threatened. Rather than keeping our focus on Jesus, we begin to think, *What if I lose all that I have? What will I do if He leaves me? Can I make it through this? Am I qualified?*

God will never extend a call or lead you to a certain position without equipping you for the task. You may learn as you work through the situation, but each step of the way, you will have the light of wisdom you need for that moment. The idea is to trust Him, to learn to look to Him and not to what could or could not happen.

Who Is the Source of Your Faith?

When a storm breaks open over your life, do you turn first to the Lord or to others? If the gaze of your heart is set on the Savior, you will be able to walk straight through the difficulty to Him and even stand amid the crashing waves in safety.

Perhaps your waves are comprised of feelings—doubts that constantly tell you that you are off track and not in the place where God wants you to be. Instead of holding steady to the course He has laid out before you, you are being tossed back and forth by waves of doubt, fear, and even discouragement. Any forward progress quickly ebbs away as you listen to words and thoughts that undermine the faithfulness of God.

Never forget that He is in complete control of your life. When you submit yourself to Him, He will make sure you are on the right pathway doing exactly what fits with His will and plan. When it came to entering the Promised Land, the Lord instructed Joshua to "be strong and courageous! Do not tremble or be dismayed, for the Lord your God is with you wherever you go" (Josh. 1:9).

Fear, doubt, and confusion do not have to rule your heart because God has given you the ability to be strong in your faith in Him. He will never abandon you or let you down. Therefore there is no reason to be terrified or dismayed because the same Person who created you and placed an awesome promise within your life also has a course charted for you to travel.

Being stuck in fear, anxiety, or dread can be very debilitating. When people give up, for whatever reason, they also give in to defeat and the feelings and thoughts that accompany this. They cannot go forward because of the fear of making a wrong decision and facing disappointment all over again.

The apostle Paul made a point of writing to the church in Thessalonica because they had received wrong information. Once they were a vibrant church, but they had allowed the words of false teachers to sway them into a position of doubt. They had taken their eyes off of God's truth and listened to the lies of men who were intent on undermining the truth of the gospel.

Paul had taught them that Christ would return for His church. False teachers countered this teaching with a different message—one that was so discouraging to this young group of believers that they began to have thoughts of giving up. In fact, many did just that. What was the lie?

The false teachers told members of this early church congregation that Jesus had already returned for His church, and they had missed the event.

As a result of this false report, many stopped working. They were parked on the side of the road and not doing what Christ had instructed the New Testament church to do—worship Him, look for His return, and take His message of salvation to the world. They were drawn off course and became deeply worried and concerned about earthly matters.

Paul wrote to encourage them and also to review God's truth with them:

> For if we believe that Jesus died and rose again, even so God will bring with Him those who have fallen asleep in Jesus. For this we say to you by the word of the Lord, that we who are alive and remain until the coming of the Lord will not precede those who have fallen asleep. . . . For the Lord Himself will descend from heaven with a shout, with the voice of the archangel and with the trumpet of God, and the dead in Christ will rise first. Then we who are alive and remain will be caught up together with them in the clouds to meet the Lord in the air, and so we shall always be with the Lord. Therefore comfort one another with these words. (1 Thess. 4:14–18)

In other words, there was no way they would miss the coming of Christ. Believers will not be left behind. One day we will be with Jesus.

There are false teachers among us today, and their mission is to redirect the focus of our hearts from the Savior to the wind and the waves that are swelling and moving around us. We should be concerned about how we live this life, but our greater concern should always be worshiping God and living our lives for Him.

The news of a downward trend in the stock market should not affect the way we live each day. Rumors of wars and natural disasters are serious events. However, when our hearts and minds are stayed on Christ, we have no reason to become afraid or doubt God's protective care. We can go forward in life knowing that He has everything in control. Nothing that happens is outside of His knowledge and ability to handle it.

Difficulties and hardships will come, but if we are focused on Him, He will direct our path and guide us through the troubled time. He knows exactly how to meet every need. Nothing that touches your life goes unnoticed by Him. He is aware of every past, present, and future event. The answer to every problem we face can be found in the Word of God.

How do you handle thoughts and feelings that have the potential to undermine God's will?

Ask God to make you aware of who is doing the talking. God always breaks into our lives with words of encouragement, hope, and fulfillment—words that motivate us to go in a direction that is in keeping with His purpose, goal, and desire. He never will guide us in a way that is contrary to His will. Satan, on the other hand, seeks to draw us off course by distracting us with lies and words that discourage and seek to prevent us from becoming all that God wants us to be. We need to turn him off and tune in the voice of God's truth because it is the pathway to a peaceful, joyous life. Therefore, when words of criticism begin to fill your mind, pray and ask Him to give you clear guidance for your circumstance and the future.

Stand firmly against any fear that would seek to rob you of the joy of doing His will. Many people hold back because they are afraid to take a risk. There is no risk when Christ is involved. He will never lead you along the wrong path nor allow you to miss His best. If you choose a course other than the one He has given you to travel, then you will experience hardship. However, if you stay on the path He has opened before you—no matter how difficult it may seem—you will experience His blessing in a mighty way.

Opening a mental door to the enemy's advances can leave a person feeling helpless and overwhelmed by fear. We do this when we listen to the voice of doubt that rises up within all of us at some point. Satan may whisper, "You can't do that. You don't have the education needed for the job." Or "Who do you think you are? There is no way you will become friends with that person. She is so far above you." Hold fast to the words God speaks to your heart.

Ask the Lord to show you if you may have taken a wrong turn. His promises are always framed in "yes." He will lead you to a place where you will fulfill His plan for your life. There are people who think, *I will launch out and do great things for God.* But they seek to do this in their own knowledge and ability. They are not living lives submitted to the Savior. Instead, they are living in a dreamlike world far from reality. Do not waste your days seeking to become something God has not called you to be. You will know His plan because over the years there is a progression in your growth and development. When you look back, you will see how one step of faith led to another and so on.

Pray and seek God's will for your life. People who just take off without direction or a spiritual road map usually end up in trouble. However, God's Word is a steady, sure compass for our lives. When we study it each day, God will apply His principles to our lives. Suddenly we gain new insight and begin to enjoy being with Him.

An entirely different world opens up before us. We pray and sense His leading as we read His Word. We also gain wisdom and understanding that we did not have before. Now when problems come, we find that God is training us to stop and pray and seek His will before we address the situation. Prayer and faith are cornerstones of the Christian faith.

Expect God to increase your faith. People who become stuck in life usually have a hard time with new challenges and fall short of their goals. Maybe they have become discouraged or overwhelmed by their circumstances.

After the crucifixion, the disciples hid for fear that they, too, would be killed. Their faith was shattered along with their dreams for the future. However, God does not leave us in a hopeless situation. He always motivates us to keep moving forward because He is always on the advance. When we lift up our eyes to Him in faith, He gives us exactly what we need to stay on the right course.

You may say, "But you don't know all that I have done. There is no way God has a plan for my life." It does not matter how old you are or what has happened in the past, God is still working in your life and wants to bring you to a place of abundance and hope. You can do all things through Him. Nothing is impossible with God. He loves you and He wants you to learn to love Him and to enjoy the company of His fellowship. Take a step of faith today, and you will find Him waiting for you with open arms.

Ask God to give you clear guidance for the future. Because God created all things and nothing escapes His knowledge, you can pray and ask Him to guide you through each day. He knows the future, and He will prepare you for every twist and turn you will face in this life.

The goal of His heart is to teach you to trust Him and to desire His fellowship and love above all else. He also provides the encouragement you need each day. He knows you will face times of difficulty and disappointment. When these do touch your life, the key to remaining positive and sure is to stay focused on Him—His truth and promises.

During my senior year in college, I went through a difficult time. I was struggling with my grades and was burdened over the low scores I had received on several of my final exams. I opened my Bible and read over the promises God had given me earlier. He had led me this far, and I was sure He would not allow me to fail. I studied hard and did not understand the struggle I was facing. Yet I kept praying and at one point even opened up my hymnal and read several hymns to Him as prayers of faith. Still, I did not receive a word of encouragement.

There are times when we must walk through an emotional valley by faith. In our hearts, we know God loves us. Therefore we cannot stop moving toward Him with a sense of hope for the future. Never give up or think God is unaware of your struggle because He knows you perfectly. If He allows you to face a season of hardship, you can be sure He is lining up a blessing to send your way. Do not give up or give in. Trust Him.

My faith was tested, and I felt at the time it was being stretched. One evening as I was walking back to my dorm, I looked up into the sky and prayed, "God, I have no business asking You to do this, but I need to know what is going on. Am I on the right road?" Then I added, "If I am, will You please let me see two stars fall across the sky?" I lifted up my eyes and looked up into a clear nighttime sky. Thousands of stars were visible, but none of them fell.

Instead of going back to my room alone, I went to the dorm room of two close friends and asked them to pray with me. We prayed until two o'clock in the morning, but God still did not answer my prayer for reassurance.

Two days later on a Saturday evening, I went with my friend Avery out to eat. On the way back to our dorm, he turned to me and said, "Let me show you a shortcut." We walked across the property of an Episcopal church. Then he stopped and looked up at the sky and said, "Isn't this a beautiful night?"

As I looked up, I noticed two stars falling from the sky. They fell simultaneously, but I did not react to what I saw because I did not recall what I had prayed earlier that week. When I returned to my room, I sensed the Lord saying to me, "Remember what you asked Me to do?"

I thought, *Oh, that's happened a thousand times. I have seen stars fall before tonight.*

Then He said, "But have you ever seen two of them fall at the same time?"

"No," I replied. "I have never seen that before tonight."

The Lord persisted, "Had you ever asked Me to do this?"

"No" was all that I could reply. A few minutes later as I tried to study, I sensed Him drawing near again. My heart was restless, and finally I knelt down in prayer beside my bed. This was the night He settled my call into the ministry forever.

I prayed, "Lord, whatever You have for me to do, I'm trusting You to lead me every step of the way." When I got up off my knees that night, I was permanently anchored in His will—no more struggling with thoughts of the future and what He would do with the present. It was settled. God had spoken to me, and He will speak to you also.

Be willing to wait for the Lord to work in your life. David waited years before he became king of Israel. There are times when God will allow you to go through a season of waiting.

During this time, you may feel as though you are in a very narrow place and are not going forward. Actually, you are advancing even when you feel as though you are standing still. This is because God works all things together in our lives for our good and His glory (Rom. 8:28).

Timing is very important to Him. He knows exactly when to answer your prayer, open the right door for you to walk through, or send the news you have longed to receive. A wise person will wait until God says step forward.

People who rush ahead of Him usually end up missing a tremendous blessing. They seek to do things their way, but God wants us to wait in faith for His answer.

Our desire to wait for His best reveals the level of faith at work in our lives. Next time you feel the urge to jump ahead of God, stop and think just how wonderful it would be to wait and see exactly how God works on your behalf. He always does.

He may not show you the bigger picture of His plan until it is time for you to move forward into His blessings. Then you can turn and look at the way you have traveled up until this point and think, *I know now what God was doing. He was preparing me even in times of difficulty for something better—something greater and right on target with His purpose for my life.*

The struggle I faced during my senior year in college

changed my life forever. It taught me to seek God in a deeper way. It also gave me the opportunity to experience His intimate care and love. This world has nothing to offer that can compare to God's personal love for you and me.

The question is the same one that was asked in the opening of this book. Will you take a step of faith and trust Him with your entire life? You do not have to spend another day traveling in reverse or stalled on the side of a road that leads nowhere. You can begin again but only with His help.

He is waiting for you—trust Him. Obey Him and He will take care of all that concerns you. This is His promise to every believer. It also is the way to shift out of reverse and into an eternal forward gear—one that will prepare and energize you for God's greatest blessings.